A Woman's SIFTING MEN

ROB ELLIS

McGriff & Bell Publishing Company

Sifting Men by Rob Ellis

Copyright ©1999 by Rob Ellis

Published in 2000 by McGriff & Bell, Grand Rapids, Michigan.

All rights reserved. No part of this book may be reproduced, stored in a retrieval system, or transmitted in any form or by any means—electronic, mechanical, photocopy, recording or otherwise—without written permission of the publisher, except for brief quotations in printed reviews.

Unless otherwise indicated, Scripture quotations are from the *Holy Bible: New International Version*®. Copyright © 1973, 1978, 1984 by the International Bible Society. Used by permission of Zondervan Publishing House. All rights reserved.

Cover and book design: TypeRight Graphics, Grand Rapids, Michigan 49544.

1 2 3 4 5 6 printing / year 03 02 01 00 99

To Shirley

They come when we are asleep,
suddenly appearing as we are
digging our pits of darkness,
pursuing eternal death.
Our spirit is touched, awakened,
then they are gone.
Only then do we see an angel
had been in our grasp,
and heaven was in our midst.

Contents

Preface 7

Introduction 9
   Chapter One: Sadder But Wiser? 13

Phase I: Spiritual Rehabilitation 17
   Chapter Two: A New Course 18

Phase II: Understanding Men 31
   Chapter Three: Foundations of Male Character ... 32
   Chapter Four: The Male Ego 44
   Chapter Five: A Man's Word 50

Phase III: Sifting The Male Character 63
   Chapter Six: The Use of a Man's Word 64
   Chapter Seven: Setting the Foundations 74
   Chapter Eight: Further Authority: Use of the Scriptures 81
   Chapter Nine: The Guilty Rebuttal 91
   Chapter Ten: The Flow of Conversation 99

Chapter Eleven: Detours 126
Chapter Twelve: Confrontation 137

Phase IV: An Inward Look 157
  Chapter Thirteen: Courting Conduct 158
  Chapter Fourteen: The New Start 168
  Chapter Fifteen: Single Life 174
  Chapter Sixteen: In the Midst of Men 178

Appendix: Diary Helps 182

Index 185

Preface

Picture the act of sifting a bushel of wheat or a pile of dirt. The sifting screen brings forth impurities. Next, the impurities are thrown aside, leaving the wheat or soil in a purer state. This is the principle of *Sifting Men*. First, bringing forth impurities for your examination, and second, bringing men to a purer state. The benefit for a woman comes from revealing a man's true character; the benefit for the man is in the service of her refinement.

As you read, you will learn the ways to test and refine a man's character. Along the way, you will see many references contained in small numerals. Many are from the Book of Proverbs because it sets the biblical standard for judging men. I recommend looking up all the verses in the endnotes of each chapter in order to allow God his say on a matter. It is a form of Bible study you should not overlook.

We know that the Bible is gender-specific toward males, using men as examples in a vast majority of cases and in a majority of its rebuke. This is simply because all the writers of the day were men, familiar with men, and women were mysterious creatures. If the truth be known, women were considered closer to God's nature than men, and men tended to model most of the problems of the human condition. From this it could be presumed that the Bible's strong medicine was intended for them. The Bible didn't leave out women, it paid them a compliment.

However, it is not hard to see that where the Bible says "men," it means men *and* women, and vice versa. As an example, Proverbs 14:12 and 16:25, "There is a way which seems right to a man, but in the end it leads to death." Women are no doubt included. In the same way, when Proverbs 21:9 says, "Better to live on a corner of the roof than share a home with a quarrelsome woman," the genders can be reversed. Keep this in mind as you reference the Bible.

Robert Ellis

Introduction

No decision in your life will impact your earthly happiness more than the selection of a husband. Your joy, your spiritual certainty, can be stolen with the wrong selection. Even your personality can be altered with the wrong selection. With stakes this high, many women choose to remain single, and who can blame them?

"Look for character" is the standard advice to women, as though men are not capable of displaying counterfeit character—as though men live up to everything they say. It's a lot like the advice, "invest wisely" and leaving it at that. Infinitely better advice is, "*test* the character," which is the theme of this book. After all, no Christian woman purposely marries bad character. She just wakes up one day to realize she is married to it. Had she *sifted* her husband's character before the engagement, she might have saved herself a lifetime of heartache.

Other than the quasi-advice, "look for character," little help is available for the Christian woman faced with the task of selecting a husband. The wisdom offered by previous generations is blocked by cultural barriers, and time has altered the mate-selection procedure so that, in the end, guesswork, fear and emotional surges often decide the issue. Divorce and chaos are too often the result.

In centuries past, a young man and woman were matched by a mature person who was not emotionally involved, who had life experience in judging and testing character.[1] Most people gag at this notion, but its basis was sound. Compare this judgment to the nineteen-year-old whose raging hormones offer a myopic view of marriage, who thinks an erection is a sure sign of love, who passes over character in favor of a heart flutter,[2] and who thinks the ever-present sexual arousal will never lose its strength.

When the practice of arranged marriages ceased, the pairing of men with women changed dramatically. Usually, the man made a formal presentation of himself for the purpose of winning the approval of a particular woman. He was on his best civilized behavior, selling himself as a good catch. He operated with a sense of male duty, which included truthfulness. The courtship process required him to reveal his inner makeup. The woman being courted supposedly tested this man for quality and rendered her decision, once the proposal was made. In this way, the woman held the cards.

Formal courting is a thing of the past. The woman has lost her role of decision-maker. Courting has been replaced by "dating" which has demoted her to a position of equality. Modern dating is structured to reveal what a man is on the outside and conceal what he is on the inside. A woman's fear of not being dated has lowered her suitor's requirements even further, and allowed the man to put forth more bluster than character. The reduction of courtship roles has stripped the woman of her means to select wisely.

As it now stands, successful marriages occur with the frequency of pot luck. With so much at stake, who can accept

Introduction

these odds? For this reason, I want you to seriously consider returning to the courtship mode,[3] a courtship which reveals a man's character and renders a woman the judge of that character. If you are currently thinking about getting married, please put a hold on your wedding until you have read this book and applied the tests of character to your suitor. You will lose nothing and perhaps avoid massive chaos.

Divorces are self-managed mismatches caused by being fooled. A woman goes on her honeymoon with one man and wakes up to find that she has married another. This book addresses that issue. It educates a woman about something she knows very little about—how to test a man's character.

To sift a potential spouse with accuracy, a woman needs a strategy, something to expand the percentages of pot luck. Not a strategy to dilute the staple of romantic, emotional appeal, but one independent of these forces, more cerebral and wisdom-laden.[4] With lifetime contentment or misery at stake, divorce and spiritual jeopardy waiting to descend, such a strategy is clearly needed.

Can the tools provided in this book be useful to assess-in-retro the married man? Certainly. And give you viable tools for refining a relationship. The only drawback is that if you assay poor quality ore, you've already bought the mine. In this case, the Bible may be a better text. However, you may find some practical ideas in this one. Your marriage can always grow, and you may have a daughter who can use the advice.

As Christians with a drive to unite in marriage, we are charged by God to make our marriages a testimony to His glory. Failure to do this approaches sin.[5] Therefore, selecting a husband is serious business. It is the Lord's business so be serious about it. To minimize the odds of marital disaster, a woman's job is to weigh the male character so a mistake is not possible.

Here I must add one further precaution. Some of the material presented requires discernment and action. Occasionally, there is outright reproof. Painful truth is put forth. Bear in mind that beneficial advice, which is what this book offers, is seldom comfortable. The way to hard truth is rarely a relaxing ride. Jesus warned us of this in Matthew 10:34-36, 39.[6] However, in the case of spouse selection, righteousness is the only choice for a Christian believer, painful as it might be.

Endnotes

1. Jer. 29:6: "Marry and have sons and daughters; find wives for your sons and give your daughters in marriage . . ."
2. Prov. 28:26: "He who trusts in his own heart is a fool." (NASV)
3. Prov. 22:28: "Do not move an ancient boundary stone set up by your forefathers."
4. Prov. 28:26: "He who trusts in his own heart is a fool." (NASV) Rom. 12:2: "Do not conform any longer to the pattern of this world, but be transformed by the renewing of your mind."
5. Js. 4:17: "Anyone, then, who knows the good he ought to do and doesn't do it, sins."
6. Matt. 10:34-36: "Do not suppose that I have come to bring peace to the earth. I did not come to bring peace, but a sword." Matt. 10:39: "Whoever finds his life will lose it . . ."

> "... in all things God works for
> the good of those who love him ..."
> —Romans 8:28

1

Sadder But Wiser?

On the eve of her second wedding, thirty-two year-old Sandra Higgins stood before her mirror thinking of the events which had brought her to this point of her life. She felt happy. Actually, she didn't know if it was happiness or excitement or relief or a combination of all three. She declared herself ready, willing and able. Her previous love relationships now seemed like lengths of a crooked path leading up the side of a steep mountain. Looking back, she was convinced that she'd advanced, not declined, with each one. Sadder but wiser was how she had described the journey to her bridesmaids over dinner, as a way of both encouraging them and convincing herself. Ready, willing and able, she told herself again.

First there was Mark, her high school sweetheart. She was a junior, he a senior, captain of the baseball team. She admitted falling too far for Mark, that she dove head first into a mud puddle. During his first term in college, he left her for the first girl he met. Oh, he let her down easy. With all the compassion of a hydraulic press. It left Sandra feeling like a cheap summer fling and took her years to recover.

Being dumped should be a very efficient educational agency, but not this time. Sam worked in Sandra's office building, four floors up. She met him in the elevator. They took lunches together at an Italian restaurant, where he would read to her chapters of a novel he was writing. Sandra dove into his writing with him, typing his manuscript, making edits, burying herself in the characters along with him.

The deeper she involved herself in Sam and his work, the more her longing for Mark faded away. She loved Sam's imagination; it was laced with romance and a curious intrigue. Sam enjoyed discussing spiritual matters with her, and he gave Sandra reason to believe she was making headway in converting him to her Christian faith.

They never finished the book. Sam got fired from his job and soon headed to Arizona for bluer skies, a place where he needed to go to free up his writing career, he told her. Sandra felt like a failure again, and now she had two men to forget.

Then Lance, her first husband, a churchgoer. A model corporate-ladder climber, Lance was solid, dependable, pre-occupied and conniving. He bent the rules from the beginning. He made Sandra his wife ostensibly for pretense, stability and reproduction. In time she clearly saw herself prioritized somewhere between his automobile and his wardrobe. Sandra hadn't learned that marital violence is foreshadowed not by violent men, but by violators—of rules, of rights, of people. When he raised his hand to her repeatedly, she got the hint. The settlement she received after five years of wooden living couldn't pay for the shattered dreams. For crutches, she took her counselor and her pastor beneath each arm and stood. It took two years of therapy to regain her balance.

Now her fiancé Bill, an entrepreneur, the founder of a small steel supply company. He was an amalgam of Mark, Sam, and Lance—athletic, creative, businesslike, a Bible-believing Christian. A good combination, she thought, especially to cover over the ghosts of the past. This time she felt more like a partner than a prop. Yet Sandra sensed a struggle to maintain her excitement over tomorrow's ceremony. Was she really wiser? Did the trail of her past romances really lead to the peak of the mountain, or was this another switchback taking her in yet another direction? Her heart couldn't afford another blow. Ready, willing and able, she recited again.

Sandra sat down on the bed. Realistically, on what basis could she claim any peace of mind over her decision to marry Bill? Had she done anything fundamentally different in choosing him? The fact that she would marry in her Christian faith guaranteed nothing, just as it hadn't with Lance. Saul, Samson and Judas Iscariot were churchgoers, too. She had done considerable work with her therapist on being a better partner in her own right, but when she thought of this a shaft of light told her this had nothing to do with knowing the core of Bill's character.

The more Sandra thought about her marriage to Bill, a courageous act considering her sudden doubt, the more unstable the floor felt beneath her feet. Had she really done anything differently in selecting Bill as her "forever" spouse? Now, a mere twelve hours before the exchange of vows, she wished he was in the room with her. She wanted to ask him some tough, point blank questions, questions she hadn't thought of until now, questions she didn't feel were necessary before. But, she thought, even if she asked them, how would she know if Bill's answers were true?

It touched off a volley of painful doubt.

In the example, Sandra has good reason to be frightened. She has mistakenly tried to believe that her experience, therapy and Christian kinship have qualified her to accurately sift Bill as her life partner. But it is a thin ruse, as her second thoughts reveal. Despite her experience, Sandra, like so many other single women, has done nothing different in evaluating her spouse, so she has no reason to expect different results. Her only true work has been to sift her own thoughts, feelings and character regarding the match-up. She followed no strategy to sift Bill's. As a result, she risks that her decision has been influenced by her deceptive, ever-present flesh, which demands she repeat the ready, willing and able mantra to herself.

Without a sound strategy, Sandra has made no cerebral assessment of Bill and weighed no character. For all she really knows, Bill could be the worst yet.

Phase I

Spiritual Rehabilitation

Become cleansed.[1]
_____

Decide to pursue a closer relationship with God.
_____

See a good pastor for a plan.[2]
_____

Eradicate the spirit of bitterness.[3]
_____

Do the will of God.[4]
_____

"Return to me," declares the LORD *Almighty, "and I will return to you." —Zachariah 1:3*

2

A New Course

For a woman, the first step of male character analysis is to purify her own heart.[5] A clean heart: 1) makes her more attractive to the kind of man with whom to be married, and more importantly, 2) makes her be able to perceive another clean heart.[6]

In the previous chapter, we briefly learned the romantic history of a nervous bride-to-be, Sandra Higgins. Actually, despite her last-minute apprehension, Sandra has reason to be optimistic. She had unwittingly embarked on the first step of a four-part strategy designed to augment her chances of marital success, that being the spiritual housecleaning she took with her counselor and her pastor. This involved recommitting her life to the Lord, *and she had to make the first move.*[7] The Lord responded by softening her calloused heart and sensitizing her spirit.

The basis of Sandra's personal revival was a strong return to the Scriptures. Studying them had revealed shortcomings in her conduct. First was her selfishness, something she saw in others but never herself. She also recognized an

> *Sandra studied the scriptural models of female behavior, how love and submission won out over scheming and assertiveness. She learned the simple mathematical equation that she plus the Scriptures outnumber any man without them.*

unholy dependence upon men for her personal worth, which laid bare her vanity.[8] She saw the high position she gave the men in her life which diminished her absolute trust in God. As a result, she made unwise compromises and lost herself in the relationships. By seeing this, she was able to transfer her dependence to a qualified Savior. In the process, she regained her Christian holiness.

Having drawn herself closer to God through scriptural submission,[9] Sandra soon became receptive to the Spirit's gentle nudges. Old habits stood out for her review and new ones were able to dislodge them.[10] Day by day she gained holiness, sometimes in inches, other times in yards.

Sandra studied the scriptural models of female behavior, how love and submission won out over scheming and assertiveness.[11] She learned the simple mathematical equation that she plus the Scriptures outnumber any man without them. This new sense of holy power let her manner grow modest in an alluring way. She emerged from her shell and reentered society, putting herself in the midst of fellow believers. And lo, one day Bill, a professed Christian, introduced himself and came calling. He or someone else might have done so anyway, regardless of her new life. However, the coincidence was a curious one.

Any attempt at successful conversion from single life to married life, or divorce to remarriage, will be fruitless for the Christian woman who does not recognize that God, not she, will direct it.[12] As Christians, unless we learn who is the boss, things are not going to be as we want them to be. Forget about a richer existence unless you first embark on an intimate relationship with God who determines your path. Failure to do this is like hiking in a thick woods on a cloudy night without a compass—much ground may be covered but the odds favor ending up further from your destination than when you began.

Consult a Bible pastor. Ask him to help you reconnect with God in a stronger way. He will have good ideas. Even if He doesn't, God will see you move in His direction and He will move in yours.

Do The Will of God[13]

Too many Christians wrestle with the question, "What is God's will for my life?" God's will for you is the same as it is for everybody else: carry out the Son's orders. When you do this, God will begin leading you to your purpose.[14] He does this with personal touches along the way that let you know of His involvement. However, be forewarned; God may plant some obstacles in your path as a way of retraining you for His service.[15] Don't worry, with each obstacle He includes a way out.[16]

Why would you want such an obstacle course? How flattering, how eternal, to have the God of all creation personally design a course filled with life just for you. Think about it. Imagine the poor soul who says at life's end, "Where was my obstacle course? I didn't get one." Not everyone sees their obstacle course. Be thankful for yours.

These obstacles are designed to help you prepare for the future God has for you. What you are being prepared for, which you do not know yet, is the sole reason you are running God's obstacle course. In other words, you are running on blind faith, putting your whole trust in God. You're running into life's obstacles simply because God is laying them out for you. You trust that He knows what He's doing, which, in the case of a single Christian, might or might not be preparation for a spouse. Running an obstacle course for the purpose of gaining a divinely selected spouse isn't the sole idea, but if it turned out that way, you'd take it wouldn't you?

Make Your Sacrifices

You'll also have sacrifices to make. In the Old Testament days, rams and calves were the sinner's sacrifices. Today our personal sins are the sacrifices to be slain and placed on the altar.[17] Be it sensual in nature, or covetousness, anger, bitterness, pride, separation from God, whatever, remove its yoke from around your neck and place it on the altar. This can be a frightening, threatening thing to do. But it is sin that has been holding you back.[18] Soon after you do this, you will experience a holy freedom that is indescribable.[19] You will own the rest and peace of repentance. This automatically puts you on a new road to a new life.

Proverbs 13:21 says, "Misfortune pursues the sinner." If misfortune has been pursuing you, admit your sin(s) and get it (them) out of your life. Turn them over to God, your pastor, and perhaps a counselor in that order. In God's economy, misfortune doesn't pursue a repentant life for long.

Isaiah 59:2 regards sin from a slightly different angle—"Your iniquities have separated you from God, your sins have hidden his face from you, so that he will not hear." Who wants to be in a position where God has turned His face away and cannot hear? How in the world is He going to arrange something romantic if He can't see or hear you?

Seeking God's Protection

Another thing you'll need is God's protection. Not only do you want Him blazing your trail, you want Him fighting for you[20] against the unseen which until now may have been thwarting your efforts. A teaching analogy is the U.S. Military base on foreign soil. If a soldier stays within its boundaries (God's will), he can expect U.S. Military protection (God's protection.[21]) But if that soldier wanders outside the boundaries (out of God's will), all the firepower the U.S. Military can muster may not save him from a hostile enemy.

And so it is with God. The Bible states very clearly that the earth is Satan's domain.[22] Thus, staying within God's guidelines, His way of living, His offer of peace and repentance, is necessary if you are to be protected and blessed.[23] If you are a single woman, you have an advantage. It will be easier to commit yourself to God's will in a pure way than if you are divided by the responsibility of marriage.

> *Until a woman searches her soul for all traces of bitterness and turns them over to God, she cannot be marriage material with whom God can work.*

The essence of Phase I is to place yourself soundly in God's will. Rededicate your life to God, lay your sin on the altar of the cross, yield, submit and surrender to the Scriptures.[24] Get this valuable work completed.[25] God is waiting to honor you.

Detecting Bitterness

The penalty for broken relationships is often a bitter spirit.[26] A bitter, resentful spirit may have come over you and is quietly seeking revenge upon the male gender. This will hang a "holy men KEEP OUT" sign around you, and destroy your chances with potentially good men.

Your bitterness could be from the time lost in a broken

relationship, a breach of faith, the loss of love or just plain no love at all. Even never-married women accumulate enough disappointment to harbor bitterness. This isn't unusual. It is the way the flesh reacts to emotional pain. To deny your bitterness merely conceals the matter and prevents healing.[27] Until a woman searches her soul for all traces of bitterness and turns them over to God, she cannot be marriage material with whom God can work.[28] Consider a few sessions with a Christian counselor, particularly after divorce, to help you deal with bitterness.

Too often the divorced woman intends to give her second spouse all the love and devotion she was unable to give her first husband, but instead ends up giving him all the bitterness for her first spouse and that situation. All divorces give birth to some strain of bitterness, and it needs to be eradicated scripturally. The following is a convenient, eight-step remedy for bitterness.

1. Make a list of the circumstances, people and things which have made you bitter.
2. Make a list of your own faults.
3. Make a list of things for which God has forgiven you.
4. Ask God to help you forgive those people and circumstances which have made you bitter.
5. Ask God to forgive you for *being* bitter to those people.
6. Ask the person who is at the center of your bitterness to forgive you for your bitterness. Pay no attention to a negative response.
7. Pray for the people who have embittered you.
8. Thank God for the circumstances which have shown you your bitterness.

> *How else could you appraise and then sift a finely tuned, regenerated heart unless you have done this first to yourself?*

We're all made of corrupted flesh which, if given the opportunity, becomes embittered over anything it can. Like the divorced person, the single woman's disappointment dictates, demands, points out the need for and requires a refurbished relationship with God. This is not to say that this will be the end of your problems, but at the least you will increase your appeal to a godly man.

Some women make a habit of choosing poor men, embedding themselves in an inescapable syndrome of more and more bitterness. If the divorced woman is wise and lucky, she will not make the same mistake twice. She doesn't need God to accomplish this. But without Him she will make any one of the ten thousand brothers or cousins of the original mistake. The Mistake family is so large that only a pure relationship with God can keep them from moving into your home.[29]

Pursue God in a different way today. If not today, then whenever you decide to redesign your life, to cleanse it of the bitterness and resentment life may have given you.[30] Forgiveness, deliverance, enablement, enlightenment, guidance, hope, grace, praise, preservation and meeting a godly mate are all based on your relationship with God. It is enough to seek Him out.

Spiritual Surgery[31]

In her book, *Knight in Shining Armor*, P. B. Wilson recommends a minimum of six months to one year for your scriptural rehabilitation. During this "down time" of at least six months, in which you are actively placing yourself in

God's will, He will be conducting heart surgery upon you. After all, God says in Ezekiel 36:25: "I will give you a new heart and put a new spirit in you; I will remove your heart of stone . . ."

Woman, place yourself carefully on the spiritual operating table. *Do not get off the table until God is finished with the operation.* When God deals with the heart, it is never minor surgery. If you have had a divorce or a painful separation, chances are you require a spiritual heart transplant, not a minute skin graft.[32] You have the very best heart surgeon. Do your part as the patient.

Study the contents of this book during your period of romantic celibacy. Apply it the day the Lord discharges you from your heart surgery. If the man of your dreams calls before this period of romantic celibacy has ended, tell him to call you back at the end of the six months. If he's the one God is sending, he'll be there at the end of the wait.

This brings us to Sandra's dilemma on the night before her wedding. She had completed enough personal spiritual work to begin another romance. Her spiritual work made her attractive, she had a right to believe that a good spirit would be attracted to her, and that she would recognize it. However, simply attracting a Christian man does not qualify his character for marriage. In Sandra's case, she had attracted a socially-acceptable Christian all right, but she was still without the strategy of sifting him.

Endnotes

1. Ezek. 36:25: "I will sprinkle clean water on you, and you will be clean; I will cleanse you from all your impurities and from all your idols."
2. Prov. 15:22: "Plans fail for lack of counsel, but with many advisers they succeed."
3. Eph. 4:31: "Let all bitterness and wrath...be put away..."
4. Matt. 7:21: "Not everyone who says to me, 'Lord, Lord,' will enter the kingdom of heaven, but only he who does the will of my Father who is in heaven."
5. Isa. 1:16: "Wash and make yourselves clean." 2 Co 7:1: ". . . let us purify ourselves from everything that contaminates body and spirit, perfecting holiness out of reverence for God." James 4:8: "Come near to God and he will come near to you. Wash your hands, you sinners, and purify your hearts, you double-minded." 1 John 1:9: "If we confess our sins, he is faithful and just and will forgive us our sins and purify us from all unrighteousness."
6. Prov. 20:12: "Ears that hear and eyes that see—the LORD has made them both."
7. Zech. 1:3: "'Return to me,' declares the LORD Almighty, 'and I will return to you'. . ."
8. Ecc. 5:7: "Much dreaming and many words are meaningless. Therefore stand in awe of God."
9. Job 22:21: "Submit to God and be at peace with him; in this way prosperity will come to you." Heb. 12:9: ". . . we have all had human fathers who disciplined us and we respected them for it. How much more should we submit to the Father of our spirits and live!" James 4:7: "Submit yourselves, then, to God."
10. Ps. 119:67: "Teach me knowledge and good judgment, for I believe in your commands."
11. Js. 3:13: "Who is wise and understanding among you? Let him show it by his good life, by deeds done in the humility that comes from wisdom." 1 Pet. 3:1: "Wives, in the same way be submissive to your husbands so that, if any of them do not believe the word, they may be won over without words by the behavior of their wives." Prov. 19:22:

"What a man desires is unfailing love."

12. Ps. 37:23: "If the LORD delights in a man's way, he makes his steps firm." Prov. 16:1: "To man belong the plans of the heart, but from the LORD comes the reply of the tongue." Prov. 16:9: "In his heart a man plans his course, but the LORD determines his steps." Ref. Prov. 16:33, 20:24.

13. Matt. 7:21: "Not everyone who says to me, 'Lord, Lord' will enter the kingdom of heaven, but only he who does the will of my Father who is in heaven."

14. Prov. 23:18-19: "There is surely a future hope for you, and your hope will not be cut off. Listen, my son, and be wise, and keep your heart on the right path." Jer. 29:11: "'For I know the plans I have for you,' declares the LORD, 'plans to prosper you and not harm you, plans to give you hope and a future.'"

15. Jer. 9:7: "Therefore this is what the LORD Almighty says: 'See, I will refine and test them, for what else can I do because of the sin of my people?'" James 1:2-4: "Consider it pure joy, my brothers, whenever you face trials of many kinds, because you know that the testing of your faith develops perseverance. Perseverance must finish its work so that you may be mature and complete, not lacking anything."

16. 1 Cor. 10:13: ". . . And God is faithful; he will not let you be tempted beyond what you can bear. But when you are tempted, he will also provide a way out so that you can stand up under it."

17. Prov. 21:3: "To do what is right and just is more acceptable to the LORD than sacrifice." Ps. 51:16-17: "You do not delight in sacrifice, or I would bring it; you do not take pleasure in burnt offerings. The sacrifices of God are a broken spirit; a broken and contrite heart . . ." Hos. 6:6: "For I delight in loyalty rather than sacrifice, and the . . . knowledge of God rather than burnt offerings." (NASV)

18. Num. 32:23: "But if you fail to do this, you will be sinning against the LORD; and you may be sure that your sin will find you out."

19. Prov. 4:18: "The path of the righteous is like the first gleam of dawn, shining ever brighter till the full light of day." Php 4:9. ". . . the God

of peace will be with you." John 14:27 "Peace I leave with you; my piece I give you."

20. Exod. 14:14: "The LORD will fight for you; you need only to be still." Ref. Ps. 41:1-3.
21. Prov. 3:26: "For the Lord will be your confidence and will keep your foot from being snared."
22. 1 Jn. 5:19: "We should know that we are children of God, and that the whole world is under the control of the evil one."
23. Prov. 2:7-8: "He holds victory in store for the upright, he is a shield to those whose walk is blameless, for he guards the course of the just and protects the way of his faithful ones."
24. Prov. 16:3: "Commit to the LORD whatever you do and your plans will succeed." 2 Cor. 5:20: "We implore you on Christ's behalf: Be reconciled to God."
25. Prov. 14:23: "All hard work brings a profit, but mere talk leads only to poverty." Prov. 4:7: "Wisdom is supreme therefore get wisdom. Though it cost all you have, get understanding." Prov. 8:10-11: "Choose my instruction instead silver, knowledge rather than choice gold." Matt. 13:44: "The kingdom of heaven is like treasure hidden in a field. When a man found it, he hid it again, and then in his joy went and sold all he had and bought that field."
26. Num. 5:18-28; v. 27: "If she has defiled herself and been unfaithful to her husband, then when she is made to drink the water that brings a curse, it will go into her and cause bitter suffering . . . and she will become accursed . . ."
27. Prov. 28:13: "He who conceals his sins does not prosper, but whoever confesses and renounces them finds mercy."
28. 2 Tim. 2:21: (reverse gender) "If a man cleanses himself from the latter [see v. 20], he will be an instrument for noble purposes, made holy, useful to the Master and prepared to do any good work."
29. Prov. 3:33: "God's blessing is on the house of the righteous."
30. Gen. 3:16: "To the woman he [God] said, 'I will greatly increase your pains in childbearing, with pain you will give birth to children. Your

desire will be for your husband, and he will rule over you." Ecc. 9:9: ". . . this is your lot in life and in your toilsome labor under the sun."
31. Prov. 22: 17-19.
32. Ezek. 36:25-27: "I will sprinkle clean water on you, and you will be clean. I will cleanse you from all your impurities and from all your idols. I will give you a new heart and put a new spirit in you . . ."

Phase II: Understanding Men

Foundations of Male Character

The Male Ego

A Man's Word

> *"Wisdom will save you from the ways of wicked men, from men whose words are perverse."*
> —*Proverbs 2:12*

3

Foundations of Male Character

Many men (and women) are bitter divorces waiting to happen.[1] In the wedding tuxedo all men look handsome, charming, every bit a gift of God, yet many lie in wait to add turmoil to the weight of passing years, theirs as well as yours.[2] All they need is a marriage, perhaps a couple of children, and a little time to percolate. They are unenlightened perpetrators, cursed with an unrepentant nature, poised to inflict damage upon themselves and whoever has the misfortune of marrying them.[3]

So the woman's trick of happiness and contentment lies in finding the *type* of husband who will fight *with* her against the ravages of the flesh, the world and the devil. A woman needs an ally capable of victory over these villains, not someone who will aid them. Finding and marrying this kind of man is God's will for every woman who chooses to marry.

The single woman who wants a godly marriage must sooner or later ask the question, "How do I find this type of man?" The operative word here is *type*, meaning that instead of merely looking for a husband, she will be judging among types of men. She will have the task of selecting a particular *type* from several possibilities. She is looking for a *type* of person set apart from the others.

Recognizing the Good Heart

Just as sin attracts sin, goodness attracts goodness. A woman's spiritual antennae should always be up, receptive to the signs of a regenerated man. Rather than becoming giddy over the possibility of dating a certain male, she should be secretly sifting him to see if he is markedly different from the sin-laden but socially acceptable man.[4] She can recognize the good heart by its actions,[5] countenance,[6] a look in the eyes,[7] speech,[8] goodness-striving,[9] the way a man does his work[10] or particularly by a man's kindness.[11] First Timothy 5:24 says, ". . . good deeds are obvious, and even those that are not cannot be hidden."

In any text guiding a single woman through the predicament of selecting a worthy, lifetime partner, two inevitable questions arise: 1) "What criteria do I use to pick a husband?" and 2) "How do I decide what to look for?" A safe answer to the first would be, "Well, more than just your temporary opinion." To the second, "Read Proverbs."

To complicate matters, the stuff of attraction and romance primarily involves emotion. So the romantic single is placed in the bind of needing to make an intellectual decision in an emotional environment. Even the renewed Christian whose mind has gained control over her flesh is in for an agonizingly deceptive tug-of-war. And the stakes are high. Divorce claims approximately one out of every two marriages.

Fortunately, the Christian woman has the Bible as her resource. The Book of Proverbs spends time tediously describing the good and the bad man. In this way, the Bible becomes a sharp tool for eliminating troublesome characters.

The following are lists of male characters, their traits and their scriptural references. These lists do not include the complete verses. When you locate a particular trait which stands out, check the box and locate the complete verse for biblical content.

Bear in mind, these lists are a tool to define a man's character, *not test it*. By straining a man through the Book of Proverbs, a woman learns to identify his character. Later, not now, she will test it.[12]

Worthy, Desirable Character Traits

A Man of Character (specific) . . .
- ❏ listens to instruction (Prov. 4:13, 10:17)
- ❏ has refreshing speech (Prov. 10:11, 20)
- ❏ is glad, joyful (Prov. 10:28, 12:20)
- ❏ is delivered from trouble (Prov. 11:8)
- ❏ has healthy desires (Prov. 11:23)
- ❏ has just, fair plans and thoughts (Prov. 12:5)
- ❏ is a good steward of animals (Prov. 12:10)
- ❏ hates lies (Prov. 13:5)
- ❏ fears the Lord (Prov. 14:2)
- ❏ keeps away from trouble (Prov. 20:3)

The Man of Character (general) . . .
- ❏ finds wisdom and understanding (Prov. 3:13)
- ❏ has sound thinking and discretion (Prov. 2:11)
- ❏ does not withhold good to whom it is due (Prov. 3:27)

Foundations of Male Character

- avoids evil and evil people (Prov. 4:15, 14:4)
- guards his heart (Prov. 4:23)
- takes his father's advice (Prov. 6:20)
- takes his mother's advice (Prov. 6:20)
- guards his mouth (Prov. 13:3)
- is gracious to the poor (Prov. 14:31)
- seeks knowledge (Prov. 15:14)
- is even tempered (Prov. 17:27)
- is patient (Prov. 19:11)
- is kind (Prov. 13:22)
- desires a good name over riches (Prov. 22:1)
- hates unjust gain (Prov. 28:16)

The Wise Man . . .
- makes his father happy (Prov. 10:1, 15:20, 29:3)
- stores up knowledge (Prov. 10:14)
- lives in a way to win souls (Prov. 11:30)
- listens to advice (Prov. 12:15)
- brings healing with words (Prov. 12:18)
- accepts discipline (Prov. 13:1)
- acts with knowledge, not impulse (Prov. 13:16)
- keeps wise company (Prov. 13:20)
- builds a home (Prov. 14:1)
- is careful, cautious (Prov. 14:15–16)
- seeks knowledge (Prov. 18:15)
- keeps the law (Prov. 28:7)
- holds back his anger (Prov. 29:8)
- holds back his temper (Prov. 29:8)

The Good Man . . .
- obtains favor from the Lord (Prov. 12:2)
- is satisfied with who he is (Prov. 14:14)

The Capable Man (reverse gender of the Capable Woman) . . .
- is trustworthy (Prov. 31:11)
- enjoys work (Prov. 31:13)
- is industrious (Prov. 31:16, 22, 24, 27)
- is physically fit (Prov. 31:17)
- is compassionate to the poor (Prov. 31:20)
- is well provisioned and clothed (Prov. 31:21-22)
- is optimistic by nature (Prov. 31:25)
- fears the Lord (Prov. 31:30)

Identifying the Creeps

In a nation where self-indulgence, bizarre behavior, overconsumption, gambling, stimulants, narcotics, marginal integrity, vice, cruelty, perversion and crime are commonplace, identifying a bad man's character becomes vital.[13] In Proverbs, we see the man to be avoided labeled many things—the Scoffer, the Fool, the Lazy Man, the Angry Man, the Hot-tempered Man, the Wicked Man, the Man of Violence, the Worthless Man, the Proud Man, the Slanderer and a few others. By describing these rascals and their behavior, the Bible strongly warns you of these characters.

A man has many facets of personality. Whenever the Bible classifies your suitor's character in multiple negatives, take serious heed.

Whenever the Bible classifies your suitor's character in multiple negatives, take serious heed.

Each one of the above personalities holds the power to destroy your happiness or even your life. They and other shabby characters are depicted as follows.

Foundations of Male Character

The Fool . . .
- loses his temper (Prov. 29:11)
- hates the truth (Prov. 1:22)
- is lazy (Prov. 1:32)
- displays dishonor (Prov. 3:35)
- spreads damaging lies (Prov. 10:18)
- will die for lack of understanding (Prov. 10:21)
- is grief to his mother (Prov. 10:1)
- does wicked deeds for sport (Prov. 10:23)
- hates to be told he is wrong (Prov. 12:1)
- refuses advice (Prov. 12:15)
- speaks before thinking (Prov. 12:16)
- openly displays foolishness without regard to sin (Prov. 13:16)
- brings down others by his sin (Prov. 13:20)
- ruins his household (Prov. 14:1)
- invites punishment (Prov. 14:13)
- lies (Prov. 14:8)
- mocks sin (Prov. 14:9)
- is arrogant and careless (Prov. 14:16)
- rejects his father's discipline (Prov. 15:5)
- despises his mother (Prov. 15:20)
- has arrogant, tasteless speech (Prov. 17:7)
- is more a dreamer than a realist (Prov. 17:24)
- will ruin himself with his mouth (Prov. 18:7)
- gives answers before hearing the question (Prov. 18:3)
- rages against the Lord (Prov. 19:3)
- is destruction to his father (Prov. 19:13)
- is quarrelsome (Prov. 20:3)

The Wicked Man . . .
- lies (Prov. 6:12)
- interacts with secrecy (Prov. 6:13)

Sifting Men: A Woman's Guide to Male Character

- is hated by God (Prov. 6:16-19)
- devises evil, wicked plans (Prov. 6:14, 18)
- spreads trouble, problems (Prov. 6:14)
- will reap devastation (Prov. 10:25)
- will have shortened years (Prov. 10:27)
- is without hope for the future (Prov. 10:28)
- is perverted in thought and speech (Prov. 10:32)
- will fall by his own ways (Prov. 11:5)
- talks about making trouble (Prov. 24:2)

The Lazy Man . . .
- is a couch potato (Prov. 6:9)
- desires nothing, gets nothing, is not ambitious (Prov. 13:4)
- talks but does not act (Prov. 14:23)
- has a path of life filled with difficulty (Prov. 15:19)
- is a partner to the one who destroys (Prov. 18:9)
- will suffer hunger (Prov. 19:15)
- hoards what is free but will not work (Prov. 19:24)
- does not prepare for opportunity (Prov. 20:4)
- is afraid of going outside (Prov. 22:13)

The Angry Man . . .
- stirs up trouble (Prov. 29:22)
- shall bear penalties again and again (Prov. 19:19)

The Hot-tempered Man . . .
- is continually aggressive (Prov. 29:22)
- acts foolishly (Prov. 14:17)
- prefers foolishness and folly (Prov. 14:29)
- has passions that are rotten to the bones (Prov. 14:30)

The Cruel Man . . .
- does himself harm (Prov. 11:17)

Foundations of Male Character

The Scoffer . . .
- does not listen to advice (Prov. 13:1)
- claims to desire wisdom but never finds it (Prov. 14:6)
- hates those who correct him (Prov. 15:12)
- will not receive help (Prov. 15:12)
- will not admit that someone may know more than he (Prov. 15:12)
- is an abomination to men (Prov. 24:9)
- causes dissention (Prov. 22:10)

The Rebellious Man . . .
- seeks only evil (Prov. 17:11)

The Worthless Man . . .
- digs up evil (Prov. 6:27)

The Naive Man . . .
- believes everything (Prov. 14:15)
- chases fantasies (Prov. 12:11, 17:24)

The Proud Man . . .
- is an abomination to the Lord and will not go unpunished (Prov. 16:5)

The Slanderer (Liar) . . .
- separates intimate friends (Prov. 16:28)
- will perish (Prov. 19:9)

The Adulterer (reverse gender of the Adulteress) . . .
- is blind, unable to see his own wrongdoing (Prov. 30:20)
- flatters with his words, charms (Prov. 2:16, 7:21)
- has divorced (left) his mate (Prov. 2:17)
- turns his back on his covenant with God (Prov. 2:17)

- uses his masculinity to his advantage (Prov. 7:13-21)
- is deceitfully charming (Prov. 5:3) with a smooth tongue (Prov. 6:24) and enticing eyes (Prov. 6:25)
- is bitter (Prov. 5:4)
- is unaware of his instability (Prov. 5:6)
- hunts for victims (Prov. 6:26)
- will bring about punishment (Prov. 6:29)
- is the means by which a woman destroys and disgraces herself (Prov. 6:32–33)

The Womanizer (reverse gender of the Harlot) . . .
- is boisterous and rebellious (Prov. 7:11)
- hangs out on the streets (Prov. 7:12)
- can rob one's eternal life (Prov. 7:23, 27)

The Man of Folly (reverse gender of the Woman of Folly) . . .
- is boisterous (Prov. 9:13)
- is naive, has no common sense (Prov. 9:13)
- is desirous of the wrong things (Prov. 9:17)

When you spot one or more of these behaviors in your courting partner, and you will, what should you do? Sometimes, as in the case of a full-blown Wicked Man, you will have to close the curtain and run, perhaps for your life.[14] Other times, as with the Naive Man who believes everything, perhaps creating some awareness in him would pay dividends.[15]

The deciding questions should always be, "Do I want to cleave with this behavior and accept the same consequences due him?" and "Do I want to cleave to this personality and become one with it?" Jesus said in Luke 14:28 to count the cost before making a decision. Be thorough; the law is and always will be, you will reap what you sow.

Foundations of Male Character

Character Equation

These lists from Proverbs effectively point out characteristics of the spirit-filled man and define the spiritually bankrupt. From them, it becomes obvious that a man's regeneration is proportional to the combination of favorable traits he possesses minus the unfavorable traits. The equation looks something like this:

Desirable traits - undesirable traits = character of a prospective spouse.

Do not marry the potential of this formula, marry the formula.[16] The sum total should already be birthed and growing if the relationship is worthy of continuing.

As a sifter of character, you will have the chance to change the sum of this equation as the relationship matures. But think, if this person never changed, would you want to spend the rest of your life with him?

You should understand and be in complete agreement with each descriptive trait from these Proverbs lists before you go on. In some cases where you may disagree, as with confusing such traits as passion[17] or pride[18] with good traits, further your homework by cross-referencing the trait with your concordance until you come into understanding and agreement with God's Word. Use a dictionary for accurate definitions of words. Be thorough; diabolical forces will be sifting you for ignorance or misunderstandings which can be used against you. If you aren't in agreement with God's Word on each trait, you may miss one and be saddled with the true definition the rest of your life.[19]

This is Bible study, and as a Christian woman you are required to do it. When you understand the traits in their context, you can use them as a check list to define a particular man's personality. Use it on each man with whom you are entering a relationship.

Remember, this is God's business, so be serious about it.

Sifting Men: A Woman's Guide to Male Character

Endnotes

1. Prov. 23:27-8 (reverse gender): "for a prostitute is a deep pit and a wayward wife is a narrow well. Like a bandit she lies in wait and multiplies the unfaithful among men."
2. Prov. 19:13 (reverse gender): "... a quarrelsome wife is like a constant dripping." Prov. 27:15 (reverse gender): "A quarrelsome wife is like a constant dripping on a rainy day, restraining her is like restraining the wind."
3. Prov. 17:21: "He who begets a fool does so to his sorrow." (NASV)
4. 1 Tim. 6:17-19. Prov. 19:1: "Better a poor man whose walk is blameless than a fool whose lips are perverse."
5. Eph. 2:10: "For we are God's workmanship, created in Christ Jesus to do good works, which God prepared in advance for us to do."
6. Prov. 15:13: "A happy heart makes the face cheerful . . ."
7. Lk. 11:34: "Your eye is the lamp of your body. When your eyes are good, your whole body also is full of light."
8. Prov. 4:24: "Put away every perversity from your mouth, keep corrupt talk from your lips." Ps. 37:30: "The mouth of the righteous man utters wisdom, and his tongue speaks what is just."
9. 2 Cor. 6:3-10. 1 Pet 3:13: "Who is going to harm you if you are eager to do good?"
10. Prov. 31:15 (reverse gender): "She gets up while it is still dark; she provides food for her family . . ." Prov. 31:17: "She sets about her work vigorously; her arms are strong for her tasks."
11. Prov. 19:22: "What is desirable in a man is his kindness." (NASV)
12. Prov. 20:5 (reverse gender): "The purposes of a man's heart are deep waters, but a man of understanding draws them out." Note: A man's intention may be hidden, but a wise woman is able to penetrate and discern his inner thoughts.
13. Rom. 1:29-31.
14. Prov. 5:8, 9, 10 (reverse gender): "Keep a path far from [him], do not go near the door of [his] house, lest you give your best strength to others and your years to one who is cruel . . ."

Foundations of Male Character

15. Gal. 6:7-9: "A man reaps what he sows. The one who sows to please his sinful nature . . . will reap destruction; the one who sows to please the Spirit . . . will reap eternal life."
16. Prov. 13:10: "Through presumption comes nothing but strife." (NASV)
17. Prov. 14:30: "A heart at peace gives life to the body, but passion rots the bones." (NASV) Gal. 5:24: "Those who belong to Christ Jesus have crucified the sinful nature with his passions and desires."
18. Prov. 13:10: "Pride only breeds quarrels, but wisdom is found in those who take advice." Prov. 21:4: "Haughty eyes and a proud heart, the lamp of the wicked, are sin." Prov. 21:24: "The proud and the arrogant man—'Mocker' is his name . . ."
19. Prov. 30:6: "Do not add to his [God's] words or he will rebuke you and prove you a liar."

> *"All a man's efforts are for his mouth, yet his appetite is never satisfied."*
> — *Ecclesiastes 6:7*

4

The Male Ego

Though men and women are equal in God's eyes, they are distinctly different creatures. Male flesh is different from female flesh. For one thing, males usually have a lot more of it. Aside from the obvious sexual differences, male brain structure, muscle composition, hormone production, and bone density all have different structure than their female counterparts. The male hormone testosterone cascades through the male body like liquid flesh. It pushes males into different behavioral patterns, behavioral patterns women cannot identify with.

Scientific evidence and observation prove that males have different instinctive patterns as well. Children as a whole are born amoral and egocentric, but as they grow the condition tends to lessen in little girls and persist in little boys. Young boys are a great deal more physically aggressive than are young girls, and they are more prone to take out their frustrations on others. It takes longer to civilize boys; a lifetime is frequently not long enough. The ratio of male prison inmates to female illustrates the point.

The driving forces in the man's personality are competition and the security it wins. From an early age the male begins working out his place in the hierarchy of other males. Along the way, his struggle satisfies his flesh with powerful perks like parental and peer approval in his early years, and later, female approval. Such approval provides powerful incentive to continue to compete.

Freud termed this competitive urge the ego. For the Christian, ego and flesh have the same meaning. Men with big egos have a lot of fleshy urges driving them,[1] and frequently they get trapped in a cycle that competes around the clock. Some men may not appear to be competitors, but the instincts are there, the ego is alive. In these cases, they compete by methodically not competing, thereby gaining their place with other competitors by not threatening them.

> *From his lonely pits, traps of blind, dead end pursuit, a man cannot remove himself.*

Balancing the competitive urges is the struggle of every man. When carried to an extreme, the male competitive syndrome turns destructive to the person, his family, and society.[2] A man in the hyper-competitive mode puts on blinders and plows ahead, chasing the idols of winning, obtaining, achieving and competing into dark pits.[3] From the load, his emotions can get parched, and his mind can become grooved into a dull stupor. This is the definition of a man living in darkness. He becomes wise in competing all right (selfishness), but is ignorant of unselfish actions.[4] From his lonely pits, traps of blind, dead end pursuit,[5] a man cannot remove himself.[6]

Typically, a man in this ego-driven state is preoccupied. He speaks and acts before thinking, overlooks details and backs himself into corner after corner with his statements and actions. He is wide open to strategic rebuke. He can frequently be tripped up by a woman showing him that what he has said, he has not done.

A spiritually mature man has a better grip on his ego. The born-again experience is one of gaining control over the flesh (sin nature) and allowing the spirit (goodness) to reign. This man will generally stop before competing himself into a pit.[7] He will think before speaking or acting. As a result, he is harder to trip up because his goodness protects him from error.

Since a large portion of a man's ego operates to impress the opposite sex, female opinion becomes a critical factor in his emotional health. By being vital to his ever-driving ego, the woman gains her foothold. However, she lacks the competitive cunning of her counterpart when it comes to relationships: her trump card, distancing herself from a man when justified, goes against her instincts. Often it is only withdrawing her affection, distancing herself emotionally, and accepting the risk of courtship divorce that allows a man to extract himself from his pits of darkness. In this way, a woman engineers change in a man.

A Woman's Effect on Male Ego

Jennifer and Carl had been dating almost four months when she witnessed a sharp display of Carl's temper. A grocery store clerk refused to cash his two-party check, even though Carl was a regular customer who frequently cashed his own checks. In expressing his displeasure to the young cashier, Carl made some cutting comments and a moderate scene laced with sarcasm.

Jennifer confronted him that evening after his anger

died down. Carl said it wasn't as awful as she made it sound, and that he couldn't help it, things like that set him off. "The policy is what is wrong," he said. Jennifer called it a night.

The next day she calls Carl to say she is disappointed in him. (A woman's words, "I'm disappointed that you . . ." cuts into a man's ego like a dagger.) Jennifer explains that her Christian faith compels her to temporarily withdraw from the relationship and seek counsel about it. The reasons, she carefully explains, are the scene at the grocery store combined with his cavalier attitude about it, the damage he tried to inflict on the cashier and a poor public testimony. She ends by saying that if he wishes to talk by phone he may, after a week has passed.[8]

Jennifer follows her plan.[9] Carl is heartsick. The words, "I am disappointed" ring in his ear. It seems as though everything he has done to be a man worthy of admiration has failed. Worse, he is threatened by the thought that Jennifer will begin looking for someone she can admire, someone who won't disappoint her. Someone who, by Carl's own male definition, is a better man. This slays the very core of his being.

Carl begins competing, something his nature does in times of trouble. He is forced to think deeply. Due to his hemorrhaging ego, he considers the thought, "Maybe Jennifer is right." His spirit tells him, "You acted poorly." He sees Jesus and is ashamed. He reads the book of John over again. He becomes convicted.

He calls Jennifer after four days with the good news. Though her soul cries out for it, Jennifer won't speak to Carl because her word said one week. Carl goes back to the Scriptures to ease the pain. He reads the Book of Proverbs and finds himself as The Fool. He is appalled by his weakened faith. He re-reads Romans and takes a fresh interest in Bible study. His situation seems to require special counsel, so he talks with a friend who follows Christ. After the talk, Carl wants to recommit his life. After all this, he wants to tell Jennifer, but he knows she won't speak to him. Instead, he seeks out the grocery store cashier and apologizes to him.

Of course this story is fiction, but not fantasy. It is a viable story of how a good man reacts when a woman has entered his heart. Any woman who conducts herself in a godly manner can have this effect, whether she is a friend or heartthrob.
It is the same effect a true gentleman has on a woman.
What is the most important thing Jennifer did? Nothing. She painfully stated her case, what she would do, and then did nothing else. Carl's pained ego and the convicting power of the Holy Spirit did it all.
A point not to miss is what if Jennifer had encouraged Carl by speaking to him over the phone after four days? Chances are he would have been elated, called his buddies and lifted himself out of his funk. He wouldn't have bothered with Proverbs, recognized himself as The Fool, re-read the book of Romans nor recommitted his life with a disciple of Christ. His conviction may not have gained all the power it needed to change his spiritual direction.[10]
More than that, he may not have recognized how much his faith needs this woman.

The Male Ego

Endnotes

1. Prov. 27:20: "Death and destruction are never satisfied, and neither are the eyes of man." Matt. 15:19: "For out of the heart come evil thoughts, murder, adultery, sexual immorality, theft, false testimony, slander."
2. Prov. 6:12-15.
3. Prov. 22:3: "A prudent man sees danger and takes refuge, but the simple keep going and suffer for it."
4. Jer. 4:22: "My people . . . are skilled in doing evil; they know not how to do good."
5. Ecc. 7:15: "In this meaningless life . . ."
6. Prov. 4:19: "But the way of the wicked is like deep darkness; they do not know what makes them stumble."
7. Prov. 22:3: "A prudent man sees danger and takes refuge, but the simple keep going and suffer for it."
8. Prov. 18:6: "A fool's lips bring him strife, and his mouth invites a beating."
9. Prov. 21:5: "The plans of the diligent lead to profit. . ."
10. Prov. 19:25: ". . . rebuke a discerning man, and he will gain knowledge."

*"For out of the overflow of
the heart the mouth speaks."*
—Matthew 12:34

5

A Man's Word

A woman who has recognized a good man has done as much as the oil driller who recognizes good land to drill by the soil samples and land configuration—but he still is not sure if the land holds oil. A woman may have discerned a man of good character, but she still doesn't know if he is merely a decent human being or a man with resurrection power living inside of him. She does not know if he is a counterfeit or the real thing. So not only does her job become recognizing the *type* of man she needs, she is also charged with not being fooled by the counterfeit.

To keep from being fooled, a woman must believe the Bible when it says the heart of a man reflects the man.[1] She cannot see the heart's motivations, but if she listens and observes, *she can hear it talk*. "The mouth speaks from that which fills the heart," Jesus says in Luke 6:45.[2] Thus, the surest way to detect a counterfeit man is by *his own words*.[3] The wise woman considers carefully how she listens to a man's word.[4]

The first step in judging a favorable character is listening *carefully* to a man's words.

A Man's Word

This brings us to Sandra's dilemma on the night before her wedding. She had completed enough spiritual work to begin another romance. She had a right to hope that a kindred spirit would be attracted to her. She was even able to sift a man and discern a changed heart. But she still lacked the ability to test Bill's character.

It is past midnight. Something keeps coming back to Sandra. She slowly paces around her room, wondering about this final night of her single life, because she has made a personal promise of dying before divorcing again, and she doesn't want to die. Tomorrow's ceremony seems to take on more importance than before. What once was seen as a blessing has now seemingly turned into a life-and-death situation.

What bothers her is something which happened over six months ago. Bill had invited her over to his apartment for a "gourmet" dinner. She liked the idea of a man who enjoyed cooking for her. Just as good, Bill made no bones about putting the kitchen back in order when the meal was over.

Being served was flattering, and it made Sandra want to respond. She thought it a good sign that he would return a favor of hers with a meticulously prepared dinner. As he was preparing dinner, Bill had mentioned having a particularly frustrating day. Something having to do with a string of botched orders to customers.

Just before dinner, Bill discovered a mess made by his pet dog, Ginger, who quickly headed for a back room. Bill angrily followed her in and struck her not once but three times, hard enough for Sandra to hear the blows as if the dog's skin had no fur. Afterward, when Ginger peeked around a doorway and looked into her eyes, Sandra thought she had never seen an animal with a sadder look on its face.

The last thing Sandra had wanted to do was upset the good start they had made as a couple. She felt it wasn't her place to show a critical spirit or tell a man how to handle his dog in his own house. Nonetheless, the look in Ginger's eyes upset her so she said, "I don't like it when you hit your dog like that." Bill, somewhat unglued, didn't respond. The dinner wasn't as good as it could have been. Throughout dinner Sandra could think of only one word. Temper.

Why, Sandra thought in her room, why does that incident come back to me now, hours before my ceremony rather than six months or even two weeks ago? It comes back because the Holy Spirit has told her that violence comes not necessarily from violent men, but from violators, be it rules, the conscience, or the household pet.

It isn't so much the incident that bothers her now, it is the not knowing, the unfinished, open-ended quality of it.

Sandra is bothered because she lacks information on Bill's temper.

What follows is the essence of testing the character of a potential male spouse. The same examples and logic are applicable to men or women because the tools needed to sift Christian character are the same.

A Man's Word

A Man's Word

A man's word is his bond. A tired phrase perhaps, but time-honored and very true. Universally, from the beginning of time, what a man says is the course he is expected to follow. When he follows his word, his character is judged favorably and his integrity remains intact. When he violates this principle, his character and integrity become suspect. Repeated violation of his spoken word renders his character untrustworthy, in default, and the man will be judged as more or less untrustworthy.[5] Thus, keeping his word becomes a strong survival tactic.[6] *No one knows this better than he does.*

This creates within each man an instinct to live by, and not violate, his word. Even a scoundrel will twist and turn and fabricate arguments in order to keep his word intact because he knows the repercussions on his personal image, his standing with others, and therefore his survival. This principle is as innate as the knowledge that stealing is wrong. Sure people steal, but the thief is shamed when he is discovered.[7] So it is with the man whose word is empty.

Whenever a good man is held to account for the variance between his word and his actions, he realizes his guilt.[8] This quality, *realizing guilt*, is the prime ingredient in judging a person's character. It can and should be used as the basis for character assessment.

Triggering a Man's Word

Few people would dispute the principle of a man's word being his bond. Thus, the important issue to the woman who is sifting a man's character becomes how to trigger the principle. Actually, this is the easiest piece of the puzzle: simple conversations hold the key.

Every time a man opens his mouth to speak (or a woman, hers) words come forth. They are strung together in sentences to position his thinking at a certain point in time. Whenever a man expresses an opinion, discusses a topic or gives comment, *his word is being committed.* In every case it is fair and reasonable to expect these words to accurately reflect his thinking and map out his actions. Otherwise, his spoken words would hold absolutely no meaning, or worse, be deceptive untruths.[9]

For example, a man says, "I am going out to the car to see if my glasses are there." It is fair and reasonable to expect this to happen. If instead he went into the bathroom and took a shower, his words would be foolish and not worth the air he used to make them. He would be considered untrustworthy, a fool (something no man's ego can tolerate) and a liar.[10] No human being in his right mind operates this way. Of course, the man could go to the car to sneak a cigarette. This would make his words a lie because he said he was going to look for his glasses. Or he could go to the car, look for his glasses, and then go upstairs and take a shower, which would not be a lie. He merely didn't declare the shower part and need not be accountable to that as a lie.

By the same reasoning, if a woman were to ask a man who is courting her, "What do you think about spouse abuse?" his answer could be expected to reflect his beliefs on that subject. A sane, reasonable person would not be expected to say something which did not reflect his true opinion. Example:

He: "I don't think a man has any excuse to abuse his wife."

She: "So you think spouse abuse is never called for. Do you mean in *every* case?"

A question like this will get further comment, and with it further declaration of the man's word. Further questioning will fill in more blanks and round out his official word on the issue at hand.

He: "Yes, I think in every case. Even if she is wrong, two wrongs don't make a right."

A Man's Word

She: "Spouse abuse, as I understand it, means a man hitting his wife. Is that what you see it as, too? Or do you see it as something different?"

He (the courting man's best foot forward): "Hitting a wife is spouse abuse. So is yelling, cursing, name-calling, threatening. It is uncalled for in every case, in my opinion."

She: "Is there any time when it is justifiable? How about if she calls him a name?"

He: "I don't believe there is a time when a man is justified abusing someone he has pledged his love to. If he's so thin-skinned that he reacts to a silly name, well, he's lost it."

She: "Then what if he loses it? What about that?"

He: "She would have the right to move out and then call the police. This guy needs help."

She: "Counseling help?"

He: "At least."

By answering these clever questions with his best foot forward, as in a standard courting conversation, this man has given his word on a number of positions. Among them:
- Spouse abuse is wrong.
- Spouse abuse includes hitting, cursing, name calling, baiting, threatening.
- A man is never justified in any form of spouse abuse. If he commits it, he has lost control.
- The woman has a right to call the police.
- Moving out should precede police action.
- The abuser needs help.
- The abuser should submit to counseling and perhaps other remedies.

By stating these positions, the man has declared his word on spouse abuse. From this conversation, the woman has enough of this man's oath on spouse abuse to tie him in knots with his own words should the scene actually play itself out.[11]

At this point the reader may wish to ask, is it fair to assume that conversational dialogue be accepted as his "official" word on an issue? The answer is, of course. A Christian is required to live by the words that come out of his mouth.[12] To a man of integrity, the words he speaks are equal to a signed document. Any person who converses one way, but soon thinks and acts another, must be considered an untrustworthy man. In other words, he is deceptive and should be considered dangerous or worse.[13] The world may not regard this as outright lying, but by Christian standards it is plain and simple lying.

Refer to the following biblical cases regarding spoken statements: the beheading of John the Baptist on a foolish vow by Herod (Mt. 14: 1-11) and Saul's conversational vow which almost cost him his son (1 Sam. 14:24-44). In Judges 16:15-16 Samson promised Delilah his word in conversation and violating it made "his soul annoyed to death" (NASV). Samson's reaction is exactly how a man of integrity feels when his word is broken. After Peter denied his oath to Jesus, Matthew 26:25 says, "he went outside and wept bitterly." What was Judas' response to his betraying innocent blood? He hung himself. A man may not hang himself over a conversational vow, but he will certainly feel shame. If he does not, his words testify that his heart is dishonest.[14]

When to Begin Gathering Vows

Remember this: dating is not just the time to be romanced, it is also the time to hold character discussions. Dates hold unlimited opportunities for conversational topics relevant to reading the character of a potential spouse. As an added benefit, such discussions make for meaningful conversation. Custom will have the man on his best behavior, offering plenty of thoughtful opinions. The opinions he offers serve to clarify his word as a man.

Assume the above discussion on spouse abuse is thorough and draws out the full opinions of the man. These opinions can be filed away as more or less complete oaths. Having carved out the oath of a Christian man on that issue, the woman could begin a new conversation on another topic.

From the conversation on spouse abuse we can see that there is some skill in drawing out the oaths from a dating partner. Typically, the key elements in formulating your questions are how, when, why, what and what else. Practice is needed to acquire the skill in drawing out a man's oaths, which can easily be developed. The wise woman enlists a friend with whom she can practice. Even a mirror or an imaginary conversation can serve as a sharp training partner.

Remember this: dating is not just the time to be romanced, it is also the time to hold character discussions.

Recording His Oaths

It has already been stated that this man's opinions on spouse abuse could be filed away as the record of his word or oath. This is meant to be taken literally.

A diary can be a special book for several reasons. First, it can log one of the most enriching stories of a woman's life—her romance. If kept well enough and in a light-hearted tone, it may one day become a family heirloom telling an important tale in the family tree, something with which to lead later generations. Imagine how fascinating to relive the horse-and-buggy days of great grandpa's courting of great grandma. Imagine how rich it was compared to some of today's flings.

A diary is also a rich source of flattery. It is difficult to imagine a man of integrity not hiking his standards from knowing that a woman he is wooing cares enough to write a book in which he has a starring role.

Last but not least, a diary can be a word-for-word record detailing a man's oaths on weighty issues dealing with the couple's future happiness. When the diary, or journal, is used this way, a woman can effectively hold her suitor, or husband, accountable for his words. It becomes the stone in Joshua 24:27.[15]

Expanding on the spouse abuse discussion as the example, the woman could make a diary entry such as this:

Thursday, June 16.
Tonight Andrew took me to Tootsie's for dinner. I think it's our favorite place, at least mine. They waited on us hand and foot! After the hostess seated us ... blah, blah, blah.

I asked Andrew his opinion on spouse abuse. He said there is no excuse for it EVER and I agreed. He said any man that hit a woman was, of all things, a low rent coward! He said that if proper communication was established, then violence would never be necessary. I said I agreed, but what would happen if there was a problem communicating? He said the best thing of all, that it was the husband's job of "being the point man" (his phrase) in the process, that he should be sort of the catalyst. He said the woman could be that too, but if she wasn't, it was his job.

Then we talked about how sometimes a man and woman can try real hard but sometimes still not quite understand each other. I think he saw my point. I asked him, "What if misunderstandings happened between he and his wife?" (I even said me and him once, too.) What would he think of trying a counselor to help us? He said *if things got to the point of communication being a problem, he'd failed and would try one. I could tell it wasn't easy for him to say that, but* he did agree *that he would try counseling . . .*

> **"What we are saying is that a real man measures his words and then he lives out what he says."—Bill McCartney, founder of Promise Keepers**

In the above example, notice how this man unknowingly lays out his own blueprint by what he declares with his mouth during conversation. His fiancé, or wife, is simply left with the task of holding him accountable to his own words. This is the formula: Whatever the man declares, the woman has the Christian right to hold him accountable.[16]

Also, notice the non-italicized words, "He said." They pin this man down to the testimony of his own words. A man cannot argue against his own words effectively. He will only contradict himself, which means he cannot win. In a nutshell, this journalist has shown the definition of being innocent as a dove and wise as a serpent.[17]

You should now be able to see the value in keeping this kind of diary. Not only do you have written record of your future spouse's word, you may be documenting precedence for future generations on a very clever first step of sifting the progenitors of the family tree.

In keeping the diary, it is necessary to know that a person can argue effectively against anything except their own recorded words. This is a staple of every good lawyer. This and this alone stops the waffler, the denier, the liar, cold. Because of how clearly a man regards the value of his word, because it defines him as a man, he simply cannot afford to contradict himself. This puts the diary keeper in an undeniable position of authority.

Notice also that the diary records Andrew's words in one factual statement after another, much like Stephen's eloquent speech before the Sanhedrin in Acts 7 and Paul's defense before Agrippa. (Read these courageous narratives as supreme examples of defending oneself with facts.)

For help in beginning and maintaining your diary or journal, see Appendix I.

"What we are saying is that a real man measures his words and then he lives out what he says." —Bill McCartney, founder of Promise Keepers

Endnotes

1. Prov. 27:19: "As water reflects a face, so a man's heart reflects the man."
2. Ref. Matt. 15:18.
3. Matt. 12:34: "For out of the overflow of the heart the mouth speaks."
4. Lk. 8:18: "Therefore consider carefully how you listen."
5. Prov. 10:31: "The mouth of the righteous brings forth wisdom, but a perverse tongue will be cut out." Prov. 24:9: "The schemes of folly are sin, and men detest a mocker."
6. Prov. 18:7: "A fool's mouth is his undoing, and his lips are a snare to his soul." Prov. 19:9: "A false witness will not go unpunished, and he who pours out lies will perish."
7. Jer. 2:26: "As a thief is disgraced when he is caught . . ."

8. Jud. 16:16: "And it came about when she pressed him daily with her words and urged him, that his soul was annoyed to death." (NASV)
9. Prov. 20:25: "It is a trap for a man to dedicate something rashly and only later to consider his vows."
10. Prov. 6:12: "A worthless person is one who talks with a false mouth." (NASV)
11. Prov. 20:25: "It is a trap for a man to dedicate something rashly and only later to consider his vows."
12. Js. 5:12: "Above all, my brothers, do not swear—not by heaven or by earth or by anything else. Let your 'Yes' be yes, and your 'No' be no, or you will be condemned."
13. Prov. 14:25: "A truthful witness saves lives, but a false witness is deceitful."
14. Josh. 24:20-22: "You are witnesses against yourselves . . ." (NASV)
15. Josh. 24:27: "See!" he said to all the people. "This stone will be a witness against us. It has heard all the words the Lord has said to us. It will be a witness against you if you are untrue . . . ."
16. 2 Tim. 4:2: "Preach the Word; be prepared in season and out of season; correct, rebuke and encourage—with great patience and careful instruction." Titus 2:15: "These, then, are the things you should teach. Encourage and rebuke with all authority."
17. Matt. 10:16: ". . . Be as shrewd as snakes and as innocent as doves."

> "... every man's word
> becomes his oracle ..."
> —Jeremiah 23:36

Phase III:

Sifting the Male Character

The Use of a Man's Word

Setting the Foundations

Further Authority: Use of the Scriptures

The Guilty Rebuttal

The Flow of Conversation

Detours

Confrontation

> *"If your brother sins against you, show him his fault, just between the two of you."*
> —Matthew 18:15

6

The Use of a Man's Word

Imagine a woman who has cleverly guided her courting conversations to include the pertinent issues involving a man and woman uniting for life, and diligently logged the words of her potential spouse in her journal. She has put herself in prime position to sift the quality of her man. Her task has not been difficult. In fact, if she has kept up her diary or journal, she will have an impressive collection of statements in front of her. Assuming his best foot is forward, the man will most likely have painted a picture of something close to the masculine ideal. But being a wise woman, the diary-keeper knows instinctively that it adds up to something too good to be true. And it is.

She knows that any man in a courting situation, vying for the affections of his desire, is prone to putting his best foot forward even if he doesn't really have one. So the wise woman knows that her suitor cannot be the knight in shining armor he appears to be. She knows he is not putting forth his true

The Use of a Man's Word

word, *he is putting forth his ideal self.* Though he has not tried to be deceptive, he has not given the true opinions of his stained nature, either. Instead, he has put forth a combination of *how he would like to be, how he wishes he could be, and how he knows he should be.*[1]

(This is where the disappointed woman who says, "He changed" and cries "unfair" is wrong. She failed to detect that her man was putting forth his "ideal self," something no man is capable of supporting forever.)

The wise woman understands that when she asks a man his beliefs on equality within a marriage on the third date, he's not going to reveal his inclination to exert controlling behavior. No, he's going to come across as the father of equality, which is duly noted in her diary.

When asked, while sitting on a park bench, about the value of his word he will tell her not only

If a man never made a mistake, he'd own the world in a month. Thank goodness they make them.

how important it is to him, but that it is as good as gold. Ask any man if his word is good and this is what you'll get. The wise woman records something like this word for word in quotation marks.

Things like this put a man in a dilemma. The dilemma is that he must do everything he has said or look like a fool (very noxious to his ego). Armed with her diary, the wise woman has the goods to not only trip him up but, as time goes by, perhaps collapse the entire courtship in one great request for accountability. In her heart, she wants to do neither.

It must be stated here, as emphatically as possible with the printed word, that this diary-keeping strategy is *not* designed to eliminate suitors. *It is not a three-strikes-and-you're-out proposition.* The truth of the matter is this: *No man can live up to his word 100% of the time* (or a woman her's). Not on this earth with these sinful natures they can't. Look at God's favorite men: David, the man after God's own heart—sinned with Bathsheba, caused rivers of blood to flow, and was a poor father. Samson, once a godly, heroic judge, was a fool with women (although he did keep his word). Saul, the anointed, heroic king, became a disgraced madman. God gave Solomon, the spiritual traitor, everything a man could have. Peter, the self-declared loyalist, broke his word to his Lord three times in less than twenty-four hours. Can you, in your wildest dreams, expect your suitor to be any better?

If a man never made a mistake, he'd own the world in a month. Thank goodness they make them. Their mistakes afford the opportunity to test their character.

The reason it is not "three strikes and you're out" is that character assessment is a process, not a quick conclusion. You must realize that testing character requires not just mistakes (the breach of a promised word) and confrontation of them, but more importantly, *the scrutinizing of a person's reaction to these confrontations.*

The test is not the complete harmony between a man's word and his deeds, but the gift of acknowledgment and once-and-for-all atonement when he has violated his word.

The pivotal point is this: Look at David's behavior when he was confronted with the truth. Imagine the look on his face, the remorse in his heart, when Nathan pointed his boney finger in his face and uttered, "Thou. Thou art the one!"[2]

David had a curious reaction which made God declare him the man after His own heart. What was it that set him apart as a man of God? *Recognizing his guilt and immediate remorse.* Sack cloth and ashes. Hours on his knees, a torrent of tears between them. Psalm after Psalm. Zero defense of himself, only remorse and repentance and immediate measures of atonement.

The Measure of Character

So David's reaction to his guilt becomes the measure of character. The test is *not* the complete harmony between a man's word and his deeds, but the gift of acknowledgment and once-and-for-all atonement when he has violated his word.

We all wish that we could be better. We wish that we could just come close to the ideals our mouths put forth. We try hard but we fall short again and again. In trying to live up to our ideals, how we know we should live, we fail.[3] However, in repenting from these failures, we win.

A point must be underscored. You are not looking for a perfect man. You are looking for a man who, when confronted with the disharmony of his actions to his words, will acknowledge the truth, and like the man in Proverbs 9:8, will love you for bringing it to him.[4] Such a man is better than gold.[5]

> *All men give their word, all men would like to carry it out. But only some men, when shown a fault in their word, will restructure their actions to restore their word.*

The imperfect man who, when faced with the facts and cannot acknowledge them, is waving red flags.[6] The extent of his defensiveness, his countering schemes, his denial, his rationalizations, his deceiving charm, etc. is equivalent to his undesirability as a partner. By using your information gathering skills, *you are sifting a man for this very liability.*

A woman should be very suspicious of a courtship which holds no contradictions between a man's word and his actions. With regard to the Fall, it is a lie. Either she has not drawn out a comprehensive line of oaths or the courtship has not been long enough to reveal discrepancies. In either case, the man's integrity remains unknown.

Without a display of disharmony between word and action, no test of male character can take place. Imagine David's heinous action minus the repentance. Without the repentance, David is just another bum.

When you look at the overview of this character assessment process, it is almost divine in its inception. You begin early in the courting process when glibness is at its peak. Your goal is to gather information, not be romanced. Discussion, the relaxed commission of one's word, comes forth pure and clean, answering the desire to create the best impression. These words are then duly recorded in an embryonic heirloom. As the courtship continues, slight breaches of a partner's word are inevitable, creating a neat, self-generated contradiction. This gives a woman the opportunity to present the contradiction to that man using not her opinion but his own actions. How the man reacts reveals his character.[7]

You may still be wondering about ethics. Is the above method one of fairness or trickery? Answer the following questions. Is it not fair to test a person by the standards of his own words and actions?[8] If not, what else is a fairer way? And finally, bringing the golden rule into it, would you be willing to be sifted by the same means?[9]

As a tip, expect a man's defense to include counter charges before an admission of guilt. His sin nature will try to equalize with tit-for-tat, as in, "Well, what about when you . . ." Don't fall for this. It is a character flaw (point out Proverbs 9:8 immediately).[10] When he tries this simply say, "Thank you for pointing that out. That is a rebuke separate and unrelated to this one. Let's finish this first, then we can discuss that."

The Use of a Man's Word

Four Layers of Integrity

Every man knows the value of his word, though not every man values his word.

All men give their word, all men would like to carry it out. But only some men, when shown a fault in their word, will restructure their actions to restore their word. Men whose words overrule their actions are the men of integrity. Examples:

In conversation, Ricky says to Sue that he's not a drinker. He may have a beer, never more than two, on social occasions. Three weeks later Ricky tells Sue that he's hungover to beat the band. Why? He and his friends spent a little time on the town.

Sue reminds Ricky of his earlier statement that he was a two-limit-max social drinker. His reply: "Oh, I occasionally get social like this once in a while."

Ricky's actions have now overruled his word. In other words, Ricky's actions are in charge, not his word. Ricky knows the value of a man's word, but he doesn't value his own.

Don has voiced support of the Disney boycott. For Christmas, his niece requests a Disney doll character. Don goes to a Disney outlet, buys the character, wraps it and delivers it to his niece.

Hearing about this, Shirley casually reminds Don of his word of support for the Disney boycott. Don ponders the situation. He goes to his niece's house, reclaims the gift, returns it to the store and buys another gift at a different store.

Don's word has overruled his actions. He cherishes the value of his word. He is a man who shows his word can be trusted. He is a man of integrity.

The man of integrity knows the value of his word, and wants to keep it intact. He will undo or restructure his actions to fit his word, rather than the other way around, the way Don retraced his actions to make his word right again.

At the same time, no one wants a man who throws around his word carelessly, with poor judgment, then breaks his neck to carry it out. A man who, in an irritated state says, "I'm going to resign my position," and then ruins his future to keep his word is a fool. Rash statements like this undercut his word as well as place him in a bind.

When you find a man with good judgment who values his word, and when shown faults will undo them to restore his word, you have really found something. This is an indicator of great character. But who's to say this man won't give his good word to something shady or sinful? Great businessmen, political leaders, people of integrity who have built fortunes and reputations on their word have been ruined by this throughout history. What will guarantee something like this from happening to your partner?

Only a man who knows God's statutes, and who doesn't want to break God's heart, has this safeguard. Not that mistakes are impossible, but a man who loves God enough to consider His heart in a matter has the ultimate safeguard to his word and actions.

You are looking for a man who doesn't want to break God's heart.[11]

The four layers to the man of Christian integrity are:
1. The man values his word.
2. The man will fix his mistakes to restore his word.
3. The man does not want to break God's heart.
4. He honors God's statutes above his own.

The Use of a Man's Word

The Reason for Recording Oaths

Dating relationships are designed to conceal information, not reveal it. The man, like the woman, guards the secrets that might be a turn off. During a courtship, the woman should be concerned with getting the man's word in critical areas which will counter and neutralize his tendency to conceal vital information. This serves two purposes: 1) she gains his word, a man's seal, on areas of her concern, and 2) by his word the man sets standards for himself.

Using his own words as standards of conduct allow a man to conform to his *own* standards, not someone else's. This leaves him open to change while allowing him to bypass his ego concerns. For example, a man is at work. He may balk at a superior's sudden order, but he has no trouble adhering to the same order he signed in a contract. This is because his signed contract is *his* order, not someone else's. In the same way, he may balk at a woman's directives, but not his own words. Example:

Sheila says, "Ray, you once showed yourself as a man of kindness. Remember the time you stopped the car to give that homeless man your leftovers? I don't see that type of kindness anymore."

Sheila is insinuating that Ray be more kind, starting today.

Sheila sounds like she has judged Ray as deficient, and *she* wants him to change pronto. She wants her will to prevail over his. If he behaves kindly now, Ray may feel manipulated. Petty as it seems, sin-infected man sees it this way and fears losing respect over it. (Men tend to lose respect for other men who appear to have no will of their own.) And truthfully, no woman wants a man to perform her every wish and whim on command. She will lose the same respect for him that he fears losing.

But suppose Sheila had collected Ray's oath on kindness. When he stopped his car to hand the homeless man his dinner leftovers, suppose she said, "That was a very kind thing to do, Ray. You must be a kind man. Are you?"

Ray would hem and haw, downplay it, but come up with something to affirm his kindness, like, "I'm kind when I see the chance," or "Not as much as I should be" or simply, "Yes."

Sheila could then say, "Me, too. But do you ever wish you could be kinder to people?"

This is not a "no" question. The woman now has Ray's word on wanting to be a kinder man.

Back to Sheila's original complaint. Now instead of insinuating, "You once showed yourself as a kind man, stop misrepresenting yourself and be that again," she can say with his authority, "You once told me you wanted to be a kinder man. Now is your chance."

Ray can now conform to his own will rather than Sheila's, since it is his word that prescribes change, not Sheila's will. This is much easier for a man's ego to swallow.

Endnotes

1. Ecc. 7:20: "There is not a righteous man on earth who does what is right and never sins."
2. 2 Sam. 12:7: "Then Nathan said to David, 'You are the man!'"
3. Ecc. 7:20: "There is not a righteous man on earth who does what is right and never sins."
4. Prov. 28:23: "He who rebukes a man will in the end gain more favor than he who has a flattering tongue." Prov. 17:10: "A rebuke impresses a man of discernment more than a hundred lashes a fool."
5. Prov. 20:15: "Gold there is, and rubies in abundance, but lips that speak knowledge are a rare jewel."
6. Prov. 13:19: ". . . fools detest turning from evil." Prov. 14:9: "Fools mock at making amends for sin . . ."

The Use of a Man's Word

7. Prov. 27:19: "As water reflects a face, so a man's heart reflects the man."
8. 2 Cor. 11:15: "Their end will be what their actions deserve." Eph. 5:6: "Let no one deceive you with empty words, for because of such things God's wrath comes on those who are disobedient."
9. Matt. 7:2: "For in the same way you judge others, you will be judged, and with the measure you use, it will be measured to you."
10. Prov. 9:8: "Do not rebuke a mocker or he will hate you; rebuke a wise man and he will love you."
11. Rom. 10:10: "For it is with your heart that you believe and are justified . . ."

> *"Every matter must be established by the testimony of two or three witnesses."*
> —2 Corinthians 13:1

7
Setting the Foundations

Dating should be done principally to collect data. The smart woman states very early on the first date, "I am an inquisitive person, I hope you don't mind." No man will, on the first date. His response will be one of curiosity.

She may also say other things when the time is right. "I want to be able to trust you. Can I?" Or, "I take you for a person who is honest with people. Am I right about that?" She may even say something like, "I'd like to make an agreement with you. I'll be honest with you if you'll be honest with me." Or, "Do you believe (or submit to) the Bible?" or, "Is your word trustworthy?" Such one-liners are good at pulling an oath from a man's mouth. He will almost certainly report favorably to them. As an added bonus, such statements can be very romantic by their subtle indication of a woman's heart. To gain even more from them, statements like these work best when they come out of an organized framework.

Setting the Foundations

The smart cookie knows her courtship partner must pass muster before she commits her heart.[1] In order to run her qualifying tests, she must first establish a foundation for her assessment. The number of topics and issues relevant to successful marriage are nearly limitless. However, five are vital.

1. His word as trustworthy.
2. His Christian faith.
3. Mutual honesty.
4. His agreement to freely share background information pertinent to the relationship.
5. His submission to the Scriptures.

Once these features are established, she can proceed with her data gathering. For example, once the man has declared his word as trustworthy, the woman is free to point out cases when it is not. However, this cannot be done until he has branded his word as trustworthy with his own mouth.

These five foundations can all be grounded with clever questions or statements such as, "I think honesty is very important in a relationship. What do you think?" Or, "I think a woman should be able to count on what a man says. How about you?"

One fair tactic, and a way to get almost certain agreement, is to pose a qualifying statement or question right of the blue. For instance, the couple may have been talking about any number of things, or a lull may have taken over. Suddenly she says, "I've been told that a man's word is his bond. Is that true?"

It is likely that he would agree. She could seal it by saying, "Then you, being a man, I can count on your word?" He would have to agree. For one, he is a polite man in the courting mood. Second, he has heard a female refer to him as a man, something that boosts his hard-working ego to no end.

Sifting Men: A Woman's Guide to Male Character

In perfect order, something which is always worthy of trying for, honesty is established first. That way any subsequent statement he makes is covered by his word. The following are examples of statements which could be used to set the five pillars of a solid foundation.

1. **Honesty**
   - "I don't want to ever get involved in a relationship unless there is honesty on both sides. Do you?"
   - "I can't afford to get into a relationship with someone who is less than honest. Can I trust you?"
   - "We have a chance to have a great thing together, if you like me as much as I do you. But if honesty isn't there, I don't want to get involved. Can I trust you?"

2. **Christianity**
   - "Lots of people call themselves Christians but they don't follow the Lord. Do you?"
   - "Who is Jesus to you?"
   - "What does 'born again' mean to you? Has it happened to you? Is the Lord your Lord?"

3. **His word**
   - "Can I trust what you say to me?"
   - "Lots of people say one thing and end up doing another. When you say something, can I count on it being the truth?"
   - "I don't want to get involved in a relationship with someone who's word can't be trusted. Can I trust yours?"

4. **Sharing relevant background**
   - "I'm a curious person. I tend to ask a lot of

Setting the Foundations

questions about a person I am interested in. Can I do that with you?"
- "If I ask about a sensitive area just stop me. But I like to know what you are interested in, what your opinions are, how you see things, stuff like that. Do you mind?"
- "Feel free to ask me whatever you like. If it is a sensitive area I'll say so. I'd like to do the same with you."

5. **Submission to the Scriptures**
   - "Do you consider yourself accountable to the Scriptures?"
   - "If someone showed you that you were living contrary to the Scriptures, what would you do?"
   - "When it comes to the Scriptures, I'd like you to point out things I might not see in myself so I can see them. That way I have a chance to grow. Would you mind if I did the same for you?"
   - "Do you pattern your life on the Scriptures?"

Let's gently expand on a spiritual conversation.
She: "I'd like to talk about something spiritual. Is that okay?"
He: "Sure."
She: "Let's talk about salvation."
He: "Okay."
She: "Good. I think it is the hope of all believers. Kind of like our gift from God for following the Lord."
He: "I agree. When we're saved, we get it."
She: "Some people believe that our salvation can be lost. I'm not sure, but I don't want to take any chances. How about you?"

He: "Me, either."
She: "Are you willing to follow the Lord to be sure of your salvation forever?"
He: "That's what a Christian is, isn't it?"
She: "I mean really follow Him. What He says in the Gospels. Even if it's not the most popular thing to do."
He: "Yes. I'm a Christian. That's what I do."

Journal Entry

Tonight, Jay told me he feels secure in his salvation. <u>He said</u> *he's not sure if a Christian can lose it, but I said I don't want to take any chances, and he said, "Me either."*

<u>He also said</u> *he follows the Gospels because that's what a Christian does . . .*

Once a relationship is established, direct questions like these regarding faith are fair and above board. Notice that a good lead in is a courteous opening.[2]

Special Situations

Whenever unusual circumstances are known, it is a good idea to establish initial dialogue in that area as well. The sooner the better. Not only does this bring the situation to light, it can establish parameters of behavior as well as glean information on which to draw safe boundaries. Examples:

"Robert, I know that you have been incarcerated. How do you feel about discussing it? I don't need to know everything, but when it feels right, could I ask a few questions about it?"

"Nate, you said your previous marriage is history, and I want to respect that. But would you mind if I ask questions about it as it relates to us now?"

"Jack, you have been a Christian for only about a year now. I'd like to ask you some questions about your spiritual walk. May I?"

Once agreement in key areas like these is settled, you have laid the groundwork for getting all the information you need to make an assessment. If the man's agreement is not forthcoming, put on the brakes immediately.

Satan's Forked Dagger

Satan looks for opportunities to talk to us, to reason with us, to sidetrack us, to inject or alter thoughts in our minds. He finds opportunities and uses logic that the smartest ten men in the world would miss. All he needs is a foothold. Since romantic partners hold sway over our emotions and how we esteem ourselves, Satan can use *him* to get to *you*. If the front door (you) is locked, Satan will try the side door (him). This is the reason you don't grant spouse or dating partner status foolishly.

If a man is not following the Lord with heart, soul and body, he may be spiritually outnumbered. One question every woman needs to ask herself is, "Can this man protect me from sin and Satan or will he carelessly construct footholds for them?"[3]

A leading question would be, "Do you know how easy it is for Satan to get a foothold?"

He: "Yes."
She (verifying): "You do."
He: "Yes."
She: "I think the Bible (specifically Ephesians 4:26-27 and 1 Timothy 5:14) is saying that arguments, or just the way a husband treats his wife, or vice versa, can let Satan get into their thinking. What do you think?"

This question should get an affirmative answer or else the Christian is remedial in spiritual warfare and needs to contemplate Ephesians 4:26-27 and 1 Timothy 5:14. More likely, a Christian will understand and agree with the Scriptures.

    She: "Then I can count on you as an ally against Satan and not the other way around?"

    He: "Of course you can."

Now she can enter this information in her journal. If (when) she finds this man reducing her self-esteem to a spiritually vulnerable level, she can recite this conversation to him. His word as a man will be her leverage.

Endnotes

1. S.S. 2:7, 3:5, 8:9: "Do not arouse or awaken love until it so desires."
2. Prov. 16:21: "The wise in heart are called discerning, and pleasant words promote instruction."
3. Eph. 4:27: ". . . do not give the devil a foothold."

> *"All Scripture is God-breathed and is useful for teaching, rebuking, correcting and training in righteousness."*
> —*2 Timothy 3:16*

8

Further Authority: Use of the Scriptures

A man declares his Christian faith. What he is doing is making a global oath covering virtually every aspect of Christian behavior. Assuming that he desires to be a true believer, this means he is accountable to every aspect of biblical Christian behavior. This amounts to a man's covenant, his spoken word to God, and the possibilities for a woman to use this covenant are massive. She is handed the golden opportunity to call him to account, with spiritual backing and his own oath, on virtually any behavior in opposition to Christian good. It is a matter of matching the facts to the Scripture which defines the standard he has broken, presenting it to him and waiting for a Christian response. If one is not forthcoming, the matter is closed with no more discussion or debate. However, the woman must apply the brakes to the relationship.

Calling a man or woman on their word, even as tactfully as it can be done, can be touchy. Even a mature Christian will get a strong urge to defend himself against confrontation. This is where scriptural backing becomes necessary.

Since we are most familiar with Sandra's impending marriage to Bill, we can use it as an example. We know that the incident involving Ginger, Bill's dog, is weighing heavily on Sandra's mind. Suppose Sandra had done her homework and had begun her heirloom, a well-documented journal of their courtship conversations. In the early weeks of the courtship, suppose she had asked Bill to educate her about a man's temper, and then asked him point blank about his. Almost certainly, he would have assured her that his temper was under control or she should not be engaged to him. Suppose that opinion was duly recorded in a May 15 entry along with a few details surrounding the conversation—what time they met, where they were, weather conditions, etc. Then, September 25th, the incident with Ginger. The Ginger incident then provides the means to confront the difference between Bill's word and his actions.

Sandra could have taken a couple of days to plan a confrontation, cited a couple other observations to strengthen her case, prayed, armed herself with Scripture and decided to carry it out.[1] Her conversation could then have sounded something like the following.

Sandra: "Bill, can I talk to you about something?"
Bill (desiring to back up an earlier oath on communication): "Of course you can."
Sandra: "I'm upset about what happened last week with Ginger, and I need to hear you talk about it. Do you remember?"

Further Authority: Use of the Scriptures

Bill: "Do you mean that time she made a mess before dinner?"

Sandra: "Yes. I heard you hit her very hard three times over something that just happens when you have a pet. You could have handled it differently. Ginger is a good dog. You could have just laughed it off, cleaned it up and let it go at that. Maybe put her in the back room for a while. Instead you hit her, and you hit her hard. The whole thing looked to me like a burst of temper.

It upsets me because you once told me that your temper was not a problem. But you lost it with your dog. I need to hear you talk about that."

Bill: "Oh, that. It wasn't a problem, believe me. I had a bad day at work, remember? You need to punish a dog when it goes against its training."

Sandra: "Okay, but it was too much. The way you went about it. You hit her hard, three times in anger, and if I heard it all the way in the living room, in my opinion, that's a temper."

Bill: "A man isn't perfect. Without a temper, why, a temper can be good sometimes. How does a guy start up a business and run it like I have unless he gets a little worked up over things? You take the bad with the good."

We can see where this is beginning to go. Bill is building a defense for losing control. He is even trying to sell his temper as a good thing. If Sandra continues to assert her concern, Bill may continue to debate her. At this point, Sandra has choices. She can do one of four things.

One, she can yield, drop it, in which case the matter remains unresolved and she is left with unsettled feelings. She will also damage her ability to confront, reduce her balance of power in the relationship, and Bill may become empowered by his sin. (The result when word-action inconsistencies go unchallenged.)

It may begin a pattern. In addition, Sandra will feel defeated, adding remorse to her concern about Bill's temper.

Two, Sandra can stand her ground and construct an argument which may escalate. This is not all bad; she will be finding out a lot about Bill's ability to argue fairly, see his sin, fight or yield to her concern. But this is risky to the relationship. Bill could make a mistake by saying words he can't take back, words that could make him feel foolish later on.

Three, Sandra can give the ultimatum, "If it happens again . . ." But with an ultimatum, Sandra takes control, putting Bill in a position of submission and awkwardly upsetting the design of a Christian marriage.

All three options are losing propositions.

A fourth option exists for the Christian. Being a woman of God, Sandra can go to the concordance of her Bible, look up the word "temper" and study the Scriptures. With small slips of paper marking her Bible, she can open it and read to Bill, prompting her case with something like the following:

Sandra: "I'm concerned because my Bible warns me about a man with a temper. Listen to this. Proverbs 22:24: 'Do not associate with a man given to anger, or go with a hot-tempered man, lest you learn his ways and find a snare for yourself.'"

Bill: "Wow. You're that serious about this?"

Sandra: "Yes, I am." She then shoots Proverbs 19:19 to him. "My Bible is warning me and Bill, I am warned. It warns me not

> ***The Bible is to courtship what the Marquis of Queensbury rules are to boxing. It is the authority on which rightness can be deduced. It is the great equalizer to a woman who chooses to submit in a godly way.***

Further Authority: Use of the Scriptures

to be associated with a hot-tempered man. The hot-tempered man was you. I want this relationship but if it comes to the point of choosing between this relationship and the advice of God, you know which one I must choose."[2]

At this point, give or take any more necessary clarification with related scriptures, Bill must become David and repent[3] or else Sandra must choose to reduce the relationship. Whichever way Bill chooses, he will be displaying his character in no uncertain terms. Sandra will have a crystal clear look at the man with whom she is thinking of spending the rest of her life. It is important for her to say no more and scrutinize his response carefully.

Of course at this or any other point, Sandra could choose to slap him with, "On May 15th you said your temper was under control, but last week it was not," and check how he regards his word.

As you can see, with the involvement of Scripture, Bill is in an unwinnable position. If he chooses to continue defending himself and the practicality of his actions, he argues against not only his word but the Word of God, to say nothing of dishonoring Sandra's efforts to use it for the betterment of the relationship. His only escape is to become David.

It goes without saying that if Bill is not a Christian, or is a Christian in label rather than spirit, Sandra's case will make no sense to him. It may even be laughed off or taken lightly and waved away. It will simply not work. If Bill is a true Christian, then he must repent. This means Bill must see his sin in an angry outburst, acknowledge it and atone for it, as well as honor another Christian's rebuke.

Such a predicament points out the absolute necessity of being equally yoked with a Christian courting partner.[4] Without this common ground, the relationship has no common basis. The use of a Bible would be useless.

In the above example, the Bible is to courtship what the Marquis of Queensbury rules are to boxing. It is what a man and a woman can look to and agree upon to make a life for themselves. It is the authority on which rightness can be deduced. It is the great equalizer to a woman who chooses to submit in a godly way. With the Scriptures, Sandra is stronger than Bill. With the Scriptures, she has authority. She has her footing and a chance at equal partnership with a male whose ego requires headship. Together, they have a chance at a marriage designed by God. Without scriptural submission on Bill's part, an incident as small as Ginger's peeing has the power to destroy a potentially great thing.

For the purposes of this chapter, the Bible magically transforms into something else: a tool by which Bill's character is laid bare for Sandra's inspection. Among the items up for display are, is Bill a Bible-believing Christian man? Will he yield to the Scriptures or claim superiority over them? Will he respect the great weapon wielded by a spirit-driven, Bible-believing woman? Does Bill have the humility to see the truth, or does he have an unquenchable need to be right, even in the face of biblical opposition?[5] To what degree is Bill's spirit really regenerated? Does he honor his potential wife's rebuke? Does he honor his word?

Who could ever imagine a mere book, a cover and paper pages, being able to do this? The Bible allows a woman to enforce leaving, cleaving, headship, love, submission, stewardship, faithfulness, tithing, nearly every ingredient to marital success. The Bible is a magical book, a weapon in the hands of a fair-minded person, an equalizer and an illuminator of character.

Doing Angel's Work

In holding Bill accountable to the Scriptures, Sandra is

Further Authority: Use of the Scriptures

doing the work of an angel.[6] Any woman holding men accountable to their Bible instructions performs this valuable service. In fact, the feminine mind with its slick memory, attention to detail and relational bent seems the perfect instrument for the task.[7] This seems especially true when considering the typical man's enormous and blinding ego, a woman's influence upon it, his tendency toward social stupor and his mind fixed on future events.

Sometimes a man needs to be jump-started. Until God's spirit pressures him, he cannot move ahead.

The meaning that a single woman has on a man's ego cannot be understated. Her leverage is strongest before marriage, when she is a free agent, not under his authority.

If you agree, you can help the process. Remember, the Scriptures are useful for rebuking *and* training. It almost seems that a woman who accepts a man's invitation to courtship *owes* him this valuable service. She owes it to herself as well; it is the way into a believer's heart.[8]

However, for a woman to hold authority over a man in this task, she should clear herself by first; 1) getting the man's word on submission to biblical standards, and 2) getting the man's agreement on scriptural submission to Christian reproof. A woman can do this with questions like: 1) "Would you mind if I held you accountable to the Scriptures?" and 2) "What is your opinion of Ephesians 5:21, 'submit to one another in reverence to Christ'?"

His answers, which will be favorable during the courtship stage, will give her a high authority—his. If not, she should distance herself from emotional attachment.

A woman who simply observes a man's actions with a wary eye, listens with a careful ear, then shows him the picture is fulfilling Genesis 2:18 by helping him do something he cannot do well, i.e. see himself.[9] If she does this in a true biblical sense, she is Eve performing angel duty.

A man, however, may not see it this way. If he is without the Spirit, he will not be able to discern your value in this arduous task,[10] which becomes a great test of his own value.[11] The rule should read: If you try to hold a professed Christian accountable to scriptural standards on authority he has given you, but his account is not forthcoming, he has broken his word. If this happens, it is likely the beginning of a pattern. Step back.

Last, do not think that you must use Scripture every time you decide to confront a man on his behavior. Politely presenting his spoken word versus his actions is plenty. However, the Scriptures are available as backing if you wish to include God's viewpoint. Scripture offers the authority you may need to challenge his resistance.[12]

Women sometimes fail to recognize the tremendous influence the Lord has poured into their lives. The meaning that single women have on a man's ego cannot be overstated. Her leverage is strongest before marriage, when she is a free agent, not under his authority. For this reason, he'll take time and care to listen to you. He will greatly consider what you have to say. When a woman marries, her leverage over his ego is lessened. (The man must have his sphere of authority and she must submit in a godly way for the marriage to follow the Christian model.) So the bulk of angel's work must be put in place *before* marriage, and it must show progress.

Let's take a quick look at the amount of leverage the single woman has. She knows the hazards of marriage so she asks a man one simple question—"Would you ever submit to a biblical counselor?" If his answer is no, she can pretty much make up her mind that this isn't the man for her. If he says yes, she has his word on an option for any problem they may encounter. If

Further Authority: Use of the Scriptures

he says yes and later changes it to no, she has the right to remind him of his word, which should shame him.

If this woman waits until after the marriage to ask the question about counseling, her husband can say no and the matter, by his authority, is pretty much closed.

Don't be afraid about uncovering weaknesses or shortcomings in your partner's behavior. If you need to clear up a matter, do so. Right cannot be confused with wrong or a penalty must be exacted. You will have your greatest amount of influence while you are dating, so the time to strengthen and encourage his reconstruction is before marriage. It's better to know now and be disappointed than to marry and be divorced later.

Technically, the only time you will have a right to make changes in his behavior is when you are single. When you vow to accept a man "for better or for worse" you lose the right to demand change. You are then under submission to his leadership. It is something to think about.

Endnotes

1. Prov. 19:2: "It is not good to have zeal without knowledge, nor to be hasty and miss the way."
2. Prov. 16:8: "Better a little with righteousness than much gain with injustice."
3. Prov. 6:2-5.
4. 1 Cor. 7:39: "A woman is bound to her husband as long as he lives. But if her husband dies, she is free to marry anyone she wishes, but he must belong to the Lord," 2 Cor. 6:14: "Do not be yoked together with unbelievers. For what do righteousness and wickedness have in common?"

Sifting Men: A Woman's Guide to Male Character

5. Prov. 21:2: "All a man's ways seem right to him, but the Lord weighs the heart."
6. 1 Tim. 4:6: "If you point these things out to the brothers, you will be a good minister of Christ Jesus . . ." Jude 22-23: "Be merciful to those who doubt; snatch others from the fire and save them . . ." Prov. 24:11: "Rescue those being led away to death; hold back those staggering toward slaughter."
7. Prov. 31:26: "She speaks with wisdom, and faithful instruction is on her tongue."
8. Prov. 9:8: ". . . rebuke a wise man and he will love you." Prov. 19:22: "What a man desires is unfailing love . . ."
9. Gen. 2:18: "The Lord God said, 'It is not good for the man to be alone. I will make a helper suitable for him.'"
10. Prov. 17:10: "A rebuke impresses a man of discernment more than a hundred lashes a fool."
11. Prov. 13:1: ". . . a mocker does not listen to rebuke."
12. 2 Tim. 3:16: "All scripture is God-breathed and useful for teaching, rebuking, correcting and training in righteousness."

> *"For by your words you shall be acquitted, and by your words you shall be condemned."*
> *—Matthew 12:37*

9

The Guilty Rebuttal

We saw in the last chapter that Bill's options for response to Sandra's case about his temper are limited. Biblically, he has only one. To maintain his integrity, something a courting (or married) Christian man must do, Bill must admit his guilt over a display of temper. If he doesn't, he admits that his previously committed word is useless. He could always argue a different meaning of his original words, but this is a dodging response. (A dodger who comes up with a different meaning to his words is usually an intellectual coward, which is valuable feedback for character analysis.) Eventually, Bill's rebuttal to Sandra's diary and Scripture must be along these lines:

"I see what you mean, Sandra. You are concerned about how smart it is to be with a man whose temper may bring you down. And you think I may be that man. I told you once that I am not a guy with a temper, but now that you've shown this to me, well, maybe I am. I need another chance, and I'd like you to monitor it. I may be that hot-tempered man after all.

I'll need someone to show me I am or I am not . . ." Or something similar in content.

Talk about a journal entry! If he comes along this way, Bill is showing the glint of gold.[1] In addition to qualifying himself as a humble Christian, he has also given *with his word* a mandate for future behavior—that being a commitment to rid himself of hot-tempered behavior. He's backed himself further into an honorable corner, the only road out being that of conforming closer to the image recommended by the Bible.

With a response like this, we can now ask ourselves if strategic conversation designed to draw oaths, and journal stenography, is a harmful thing.

It should come as no surprise that some men simply cannot apologize. Men who love strife cannot do it. By all means, gauge the quality of any apology.

It should be clear that Christian service of the highest order has been conducted on Sandra's part. Iron is sharpening iron[2] and her love is being revealed in a godly rebuke. According to James 5:20,[3] were Sandra to have embarked on such a cause, no higher service could be bestowed upon a fellow Christian. Bill can embark on a fast track route conforming to the Image which he couldn't have possibly taken himself.

Of course, Bill could also say, "You know something, Sandra? I've re-thought this whole thing. Once I was flattered by your diary, that you would think so much of me to write about our relationship. Not any more. I don't like the idea of writing down what I say so that you can trip me up. I don't need this. I'm calling it quits" or something similar.[4] In which case, Sandra has saved herself a lifetime of turmoil and chaos, most likely. All she needs is to submit to his lead.

The Guilty Rebuttal

Grading a Man's Responses to Confrontation

A Excellent. Listens closely.[5] Agrees with your view of things, sincere apology to you and/or God, immediate or promised change, no excuses.[6]

B Good. Acknowledgment of your concern, some apology or repentance, agreement to change.

C Average. Reasonable listening to your case, some debate or clarification over your concern, somewhat hollow apology clouded with defensive reasoning, hints at change.

D Poor. Poor listening skills, debate over your concern and view of things, fear of apology, stubborn attitude.

E Failure. You're wrong/he's right attitude, talk more than listening, tries to make you feel like apologizing, refuses to consider change.

False Repentance

Do not be fooled by or accept false repentance. To a Christian, false repentance is another broken oath. When a man is confronted by facts in opposition to biblical standards, the quality of his response is a direct view of his Christian character. If the view isn't good, back off.

Lip Service

Don't be taken in by a standard apology devoid of substance. Since they know the value of a man's word, men can be very good at offering a quick one to settle the issue. Lip service is a small courtesy without meaning or remorse. When a man gives lip service, he has no more intention of changing his behavior than he does skipping his next meal.

You can tell lip service from a genuine apology by the following:

1. There is no clarification of your position.

2. There is no concern about how or why you are bringing up the issue.
3. You get the feeling that you could have brought up any issue and gotten the same apology.
4. The apology includes such standards as, "Sorry about that"; "My fault"; "Hey, I'll get better"; "I know it, I messed up"; "I'm bad", etc.
5. You have the feeling he wants to get it over and move on to something else ASAP.
6. You feel patronized.

At the least, the man should clarify your position and reflect your concern. It is good when he reacts as though he is realizing something for the first time. His response should have no hurry to it, and it is best when it includes a promised remedy for change, which is another oath.

If a woman feels she is being patronized by lip service, she should say so. Feel free to tell him you suspect lip service, no remorse, no enlightenment, no concern on his part, or a line of patent apology. This gives him the opportunity to reconsider on the spot.

If you sense that you are paired with a man who cannot apologize sincerely and follow it up, consider backing away from the relationship permanently.

It should come as no surprise that some men simply cannot apologize. Men who love strife cannot do it. By all means, gauge the quality of any apology. Though you are free to accept any apology, if it lacks a sincere quality, test the new behavior. If there is no new behavior, run another confrontation if necessary, using his apology as his oath. If you sense that you are paired with a man who cannot apologize sincerely and follow it up, consider backing away from the relationship permanently.[7]

Four Rules to Use Against Broken Oaths
1. Confrontation[8.] (See chapter twelve)
2. Expect atonement and repentance
3. Forgive
4. If repentance is not forthcoming, distance yourself with an explanation[9]

Detachment

If a woman decides to step back from the relationship for any reason, she has a Christian obligation to explain her decision thoroughly to her partner.[10] In a case of backing away, you have valuable feedback for this man. Let him know the sound reasons you have for distancing yourself from the relationship.[11] This gives him something valuable to contemplate. The use of Scripture along with your explanation is an excellent way of explaining yourself.

Example: "Jim, I'm stepping back because you are too defensive for me. You feel the need to defend yourself or build yourself up so much we can't relate on an emotional level. Let me read a couple verses of Scripture to let you know what I mean . . ."

Allowing a man to guess why you are backing away is extremely damaging because he will never guess the right reason. He will simply pick the weakest link of his self-image ("my hair is thinning") and reinforce its hold over him. A Christian woman cannot allow this. If you need Scripture to help you step back, it is always available.

Other examples:

> She: "Pete, you don't listen the way I need a person to listen to me. It sounds like nothing sinks in. It seems like you don't have the discipline it takes to listen.

There is this need to be right in you that won't accept what I have to say."
He: "Well, I can do better."
She: "If you can, that's good. But I'm backing away just the same."

She: "You swear too much for me, Eric. You said you would stop and you haven't."

She: "Norm, I have to step back from this relationship. I'm no longer comfortable around you. The refinement I expect in a Christian man isn't there. We've talked about your language and your appearance. I'm not comfortable with where you are at in these. Proverbs 27:22 says I can't remove you from your ways, so please let me step back."

She: "Larry, I need to take a couple steps back from this relationship. I feel pressured for physical contact and I asked that this not happen. You once told me you didn't want to break God's heart, and that includes our sexual contact. I need to step back. I don't feel like I'm being treated as the weaker vessel. More than this, *I* don't want to break God's heart."

She: "I've pointed out several places where your selfishness interferes with our relationship, but there doesn't seem to be any progress. I'm not comfortable being a part of that."

She: "It's frustrating that whenever we talk about your background, your development as a person, you cut it off. There is no openness there. Sometimes I feel that

The Guilty Rebuttal

something is there that you don't want me to know, and that makes me feel nervous."

The explanation need not be long but it should be accurate. A Christian man should have the humility to be accepting. If you have chosen to pair off with a man who is not accepting of your position, this was a mistake.

Sometimes a woman will not have a good explanation for her decision to back away from a relationship. She may just "feel" like getting out. This is her prerogative, but one would have to wonder about her reasons for entering such a relationship in the first place.

Sandra's mind continued to drift ahead to the ceremony. She could see the chapel, the gathering of people, Bill in his tuxedo, family members together, the minister and others. Was it a marriage or a funeral?

She at least felt good about choosing a Christian man, and he choosing her. Bringing God in with the ceremony, this time as the Lord of both their lives, would be the fresh start she is after. The ceremony, the marriage sacrament, a man of God mediating between God and she and Bill. It reassured her.

Then the evil balance gathered its weight and fell like an anvil. It was the time Sandra brought up the subject of fasting to Bill as they were reading the Bible together. She said she had tried it a couple of times. "It gave me a headache and I never got through the day, but I wouldn't mind trying it again," she told him.

Bill cut her short, saying it was something outdated and obscure, that nobody really fasted. He said it was unhealthy, a foolish thing that went out with the sacrifices. Sandra felt foolish. Bill wanted to talk about the good Samaritan parable instead, and found it in his Bible before Sandra could find anything about fasting.

Doubt now caused her to wonder, if he can consider one holy sacrament a foolish thing, couldn't he another just as quickly? Like marriage? How could I let him interpret the Bible that way? How did I let him get away with that so easily?

Endnotes

1. Prov. 15:31: "He who listens to a life-giving rebuke will be at home among the wise."
2. Prov. 27:17 (reverse gender): "As iron sharpens iron, so one man sharpens another."
3. Js. 5:20: ". . . Whoever turns a sinner from the error of his way will save him from death and cover over a multitude of sins."
4. Prov. 15:12: "A mocker resents correction; he will not consult the wise." Prov. 28:1: "The wicked man flees though no one pursues . . ."
5. Prov. 15:31: "He who listens to a life-giving rebuke will be at home among the wise."
6. Prov. 24:26: "An honest answer is like a kiss on the lips."
7. Prov. 29:1: "A man who remains stiff-necked after many rebukes will suddenly be destroyed—without remedy."
8. Titus 3:10: "Warn a divisive person once, and then warn him a second time."
9. Titus 3:10: ". . . After that, have nothing to do with him."
10. Prov. 24:11-12: "Rescue those being led away to death; hold back those staggering toward slaughter. If you say, 'But we knew nothing about this,' does not he who guards your life know it? Will he not repay each person according to what he has done?"
11. Prov. 31:9a: "Speak up and judge fairly." Prov. 26:5: "Answer a fool according to his folly, or he will be wise in his own eyes."

> *"Does not the ear test words as the tongue tastes food?"*
> —Job 12:11

10
The Flow of Conversation

Evaluating potential mates through oath-gathering discussions will be the most important conversations you will ever conduct. Take your time, chose your words, listen as though your life depended on it and be accurate in your journal entries.

The following examples will help you formulate your conversations, diary entries and gentle confrontations. The issues a couple discusses should be covered as thoroughly as possible with follow-up and clarifying questions. Of course, if further doubt remains, the topic can be brought up in later conversations. However, several start-and-stop discussions can sound like an interrogation and may cause annoyance and/or pat answers, which undercut the light conversation needed during a courtship.

If you don't get a journal full of oaths at each conversation, don't be disappointed. You only need one or two solid oaths per date to accumulate a library of oaths after just a brief courtship. Remember, the oaths flow naturally out of a conversation from leading questions. They never need to be forced out.

As you read the conversation examples, bear in mind that constructing whole conversations is beyond the scope and intent of this book. It is hoped that these condensed conversations will familiarize you with the information-gathering process and journal recording of such.

Conversation #1

Jill (lead in): "I've always profited from my faith. It has become the most important thing in my life. What has your faith meant to you?"

Paul (best foot forward): "My faith is very important to me, too."

Jill (repeat): "What does it mean to you?"

Paul: "To me, it has meant a better way to live. I look at myself when I wasn't so close to God and, well, it sure is a lot better now."

Jill (pressing on): "What is different?"

[NOTE: If the person begins backing off spiritual discussions with something like, "Too many to mention. Would you like to go some place else?" or "It's kind of personal," it is not a good sign. Almost universally, a true Christian can't wait to talk about his or her faith.]

Paul: "I have a peace I never had before. I used to worry and fret about everything—what if my job gets terminated, what do people think of me, what if I'm not a huge success, stuff like that. I can't say that those things don't matter anymore, but I have a peace about them now."

Jill (connecting): "Me, too. I used to worry about . . . (blah, blah). Would you say you have a relationship with God now?"

The Flow of Conversation

Paul: "Definitely. We talk all the time, in prayer."
Jill: "Isn't prayer a special thing? I pity those people who aren't close enough to God to talk with Him. Or read about Him. Some of these things in the Bible don't make a lot of sense at first. For awhile I didn't know the Bible was the true Word of God."
Paul: "Yeah, me too. It took a while to understand it."
Jill: "How about now? Do you believe it is God's Word?"
Paul: "No doubt."
Jill: "I think it is smarter than any of us. Let me ask you this. If you tended to see things one way but the Bible said something different, what would you do?"
Paul: "I'd have to side with the Bible. I know it's smarter than I am."
Jill (clarifying and restating): "It's smarter than you are. That means you would yield to the Scriptures?"
Paul: "I would have to."
Jill: "I feel the same way. I think this, the Bible can be sort of a rule book on a person's behavior, on a couple's behavior, for that matter."
Paul: "So do I."
Jill: "How important do you think going to church is?"
Paul: "Well, that's where I began to learn about Christian people. Before I became one I believed in the stereotypical Christian, sort of an Amish-type person. I saw what a Christian really was."
Jill (clarifying): "So going to church was pretty important to the development of your faith?"
Paul: "Very."
Jill: "Did you learn more about the Scriptures?"
Paul: "Yes. That and actually reading the Bible made things come together pretty well."

Jill (solidifying): "Do you plan on going to church on a regular basis?"
Paul: "I have to. I'd be missing out if I didn't."
Jill (shifting focus): "Do you have a favorite verse?"
Paul: "Lots of them. How about you? What's your favorite?"
Jill: "I like Romans 8:28. 'All things work together for good to those who love the Lord.' And the next one, Romans 8:29: 'So that we may be conformed to the image of the Son.' Do you think it is important to conform to the image of Christ?"
Paul: "Very important."
Jill: "Are you trying to do that, too?"
Paul: "Sure. That's what it's all about."
Jill (still pressing): "I mean you. Are you trying to conform to the image of Christ like it says?"
Paul: "As much as I can. It's not easy, though."

Journal Entry

Friday, November 9th

Paul and I took in a movie, "Oliver Twist." It was okay. After, we went to Casey's for coffee. We split a piece of apple pie, separate forks. Paul and I talked about a lot of things. He was able to open up and for the first time tell me more about his life as a Christian man. He said some really encouraging things. He left me with no doubt that he is a Christian, and he said his faith was very important to him. He's had some rough times, a lousy high school experience and parents that didn't do much good for him. Once they even . . . (blah, blah). He didn't elaborate any more and I didn't ask. I figure whatever it was is in the past and that I would leave it there. As a result though he said living as a

The Flow of Conversation

> *Christian is a much better way to live.* He said *he had peace.* He said *he prays a lot now, and when I asked him if he had a real relationship with God* he said *he definitely did! And get this. When I asked him if he believed that the Bible was the true Word, know what he said? "No Doubt!" Can you believe it?*
>
> *I could tell that he wanted to talk, almost like he wanted to give a small testimony.* He even said *that if there was a difference between what he thought and what the Bible said* he would allow it to overrule him. He said he knew the Bible was smarter than he was. *I think the Holy Spirit has touched him all right. When I slipped in about the Bible being a rule book for a couple* he agreed *with me. Oh, I'm so happy for him.*
>
> *He asked me what my favorite Bible verse was and I told him Romans 8:28-29. I asked him if he was trying to conform to the image of Christ and* he said, *"As much as I can."*
>
> *When I asked him about regular church attendance I saw him squirm in his chair a little, but* he said *that was where he learned how to be a Christian and that it was a good place to learn more about the Scriptures. Both helped his Christian development.*
>
> *After leaving Casey's we . . .*

With an entry like this, Jill has gained and recorded Paul's word and oath on a number of Christian topics. Should Jill and Paul continue as a couple, she has put herself in great position to hold him accountable in a number of ecumenical matters using his own testimony.

Christians know the sometimes overwhelming pressure on every man or woman to backslide.[1] Should Jill discover that this is happening to Paul she can become his angel. Armed with diary and Scripture, all that remains is to execute her godly assignment.

For the purpose of illustration, let's say that Paul is in spiritual trouble, and Jill is in position to do something about it. Again, armed with Scripture, a woman (or wife) carries authority over a man (husband) who is in violation of it.

Responding to her concern about Paul's backsliding behavior, Jill does her homework by re-reading her journal entries. This done, she presents her case.

Jill: "Paul, I need to talk to you about something."
Paul: "What?"
Jill: "I need to talk to you as a Christian sister, and also as someone who has grown to care about you quite a bit."
Paul: "Shoot."
Jill: "I'm concerned because I think you're falling below the Christian standards you have set for yourself."
Paul: "What do you mean?"
Jill: "Well, I've noticed some things that maybe you don't see, or maybe you do."
Paul: "Like what?"
Jill: "Like sometimes I feel you've been short with me. Like you have other things on your mind. You don't seem as interested in my side of things."
Paul: "Okay, I'll do better. Things have been rough lately. You know that."
Jill: "Let's leave me out of it for now. For some time you've been talking about the people at work pretty rough. And your customers. Yesterday you called one of them a dumb son of a bitch."
Paul: "Well, he was. A troublemaker if there ever was one. I told you what he did."

Jill: "He's just a person. He probably hasn't got what we have, and he has no choice. You don't know what is going on in his life. As a Christian, it's not right to call people who are your customers a dumb SOB no matter what."

[Paul waves it away and looks around.]

Jill: "You told me once that you were trying to conform to the image of Christ."

Paul: "I did?"

Jill: "Yes, you did. And calling a customer an SOB isn't even trying."

Paul: "I don't remember. And besides, you don't do something like that over night."

Jill: "We were at Caseys, having coffee after seeing "Oliver Twist." The time we split a slice of apple pie together. You asked me what my favorite Bible verse was and I told you Romans 8:28 and 29, 'so that we may be conformed to His image.' I asked you if that's what you were trying to do and you said, 'As much as I can.'"

Snared by his own words, Paul is faced with the truth. He's at the loathsome juncture of having to argue against himself or concede that his word is shaky, something no man wants to do. Or, he could call Jill a liar, which would gore, and probably cancel, the relationship. His options are limited. If he chooses further denying responses, the man in him will know that poor character is on display. He could do this by saying something like, "If I don't remember saying anything like that, how do you?" or, "Can you prove it?" to which Jill has every right to say, "It is in my diary" or, "I am giving you your word as you gave it to me on November 9th." He could burrow himself deeper yet with responses like, "I think your diary is a poor idea" or, "You must have had it wrong" or even, "I don't like you for doing this to me," all of which are red flags. In which case Jill would have to emotionally back off at least a step or two from Paul, which may require nothing short of Christian courage.

On the other hand, here is a perfect opportunity for Paul to display his character. He could do this with responses like, "You're right. I did say that. I'm sure not conforming very well, am I?" or simply, "You got me." He could show even more by saying something like, "Thank you for pointing that out. I couldn't see it. I don't have any right to call anyone an SOB. Maybe I'm the SOB here."

Someone who can respond like this is someone who can be worked with, who has the Holy Spirit upon him, who is gold, albeit slightly in need of regular buffing—but surely someone who is already conforming to the Image.

The important thing to remember here is that character, contrition, humility, scriptural submission, etc. can be revealed only by someone who is in possession of them. If that person is not in possession of good character, it simply cannot come out.

Bear in mind that Jill also has the goods to gently confront Paul on several additional faith issues as well—church attendance, adherence to the Scriptures, yielding to the Word of God, and all the implications of Romans 8:29, compliments of her November 9th journal entry.

It is valuable to know that virtually any Bible verse which a man recites, claims to live by, or even comments favorably upon, can be held up as a standard of his conduct. This is but one of the reasons why a couple is wise to study the Scriptures and participate in Christian activities together.

Having such weighty material gives Jill two advantages.

The Flow of Conversation

One, with her foot in the door, Jill can do a thorough house cleaning, tying in other breaches of faith which may be untended. Two, with the sheer volume of his oaths accurately noted, Jill becomes someone Paul will hesitate to cross in matters of faith, keeping him accountable. Jill has established her authority without having to compromise her position of submission in the relationship. This is Matthew 10:16 in action.

Is Jill sinning in any way? Hardly. She is being a splendid helper of the highest order. As an added benefit, she would be increasing a righteous man's love for her,[2] doing angel's work, and getting a smile from God all at the same time.[3]

It is valuable to know that virtually any Bible verse which a man recites, claims to live by, or even comments favorably upon can be held up as a standard of his conduct. This is but one of the reasons why a couple is wise to study the Scriptures and participate in Christian activities together. I know of a very wise woman who ushered the object of her affections to a premarital seminar which had them stand, read pledges to one another and sign them, making them signed oaths. The pledges were on honoring, fidelity, love, kindness, etc. She keeps them close to her diary.

By way of a tip, a man often speaks without thinking, shoots from the hip, is slipshod in his record-keeping (rare is the man who keeps a journal), is given to self-aggrandizement[4] and is so blinded by ego concerns that a woman with the least bit of wisdom should be able to gain full control of the situation by simply keeping her mouth shut, her ears and eyes open and having the courage to voice her observations in a non-threatening manner. That is, so long as she isn't on the same trip.

As an illustration, one wise woman in a group of four women was introduced to a particular Christian man. Probably due to the stimulating situation, the man came across with much bravado, cocksureness and more than a dash of conceit.

In other words, his ego was on display. Three of the women were put off with apparent good reason. The fourth woman, however, wasn't. She opened herself up to him and they began dating. Her reason? With all his tall bravado, she saw a man who could be leveled quite easily with a few choice observations,[5] some backed by Scripture. It was worth a sift. This she went about doing very diligently. By taking time with him, which no one else wanted to do, she gained a foothold in his heart. He was forced by the Bible in her hand to forfeit the upper-hand demeanor. In the process, he had no choice but to conform to real marriage material. Today, as a married woman, she is quite secure in running her household as she pleases without ego intrusion from him.[6] As a bonus, she still has the cocksureness with which he makes a comfortable living. And, he is a better man. One wise woman.

That being said, let's turn to the next example.

Following a biblical prescription for the selection of her husband, Michelle has discovered a bitter streak in Andy, her forty-year-old suitor of four months. Whenever Andy participates in family functions, a personality change overtakes him. During these times Michelle has pinpointed an undercurrent of bitterness toward his father that spills over to everyone. Tension is in the air. Several things concern her—Andy's discontent; the sin of bitterness; the open, emotional wound regarding his father and the malignant possibilities of bitterness on a future marriage. She doesn't want to marry bitterness. She decides to confront him.

> Michelle (armed and ready): "Andy, we need to talk about something. We agreed that whenever one of us has something on our minds about the relationship, we have the right to bring it up, didn't we?"
>
> Andy (obligated to act on an earlier pledge): "Yes, we did."

The Flow of Conversation

Michelle: "Good, I have something. I've noticed a pattern you fall into whenever you spend time with your parents. I've seen you get in a bad mood where nothing is right, nothing is good, for days sometimes. You're much different in a negative way."
Andy (angry): "Why didn't you say something sooner then?"
Michelle: "I'm saying it now."
Andy: "Okay, just what have I done?"
Michelle: "You're in a shell, not really responsive. I've noticed sarcasm directed at me, like when I called you to say I'd be late. You said, 'If you're going to be late, just forget the whole thing.' When my being late wouldn't affect anything."
Andy (sarcastic): "I didn't know you were so sensitive."
Michelle: "Or that for instance."
Andy: "Touchy, aren't we?"
Michelle: "I'd like you to explain it so I'm not jumping to conclusions."
Andy: "Sounds like you already have. Look, I don't know why but I just get tense around my parents. They and I have been like this for years, so it isn't news of any kind. What am I supposed to do, say no every time I have to go see them?"
Michelle: "I just want to know if this can be fixed or if you are going to get like this every time, forever."
Andy: "Who knows?"
Michelle: "It's the bitterness, Andy. I don't know if you're willing to fix it."
Andy: "Huh? When was I bitter?"
Michelle: "In my opinion, you are bitter when you talk about your father. Sarcasm is right next to bitterness

on the scale, Andy, and you have used it on me."
Andy: "Leave then."
Michelle: "Is this a rational talk with two people trying, Andy?"
[Andy is silent.]
Michelle: "You agreed that if either one of us has a problem in the relationship, we would talk about it with love as two Christian people. As adults. Do you remember when we said that?"
Andy: "Yeah."
Michelle: "Well, I think that should happen."
Andy: "Well, me too. We'll talk about it."
Michelle: "You told me you were no longer bitter toward anyone, including your father. Those were your words. Do you remember them?"
Andy: "Huh?"
Michelle: "Is that your answer?"
Andy: "To what?"
Michelle: "This is getting nowhere. You're not doing anything you said you would do."
Andy: "I've had trouble with my father for years. Do you expect me to be Miss Congeniality after I have to spend time with him?"
Michelle: "You are bitter, aren't you?"
Andy: "If that qualifies me as bitter, then put me down as bitter."
Michelle: "Okay. And I'll put you down for not telling the truth, either. Remember the day we walked around the lake? We stopped into the Kava House for hot chocolate. You told me about your family and how everything was difficult. I asked you if you had any bitterness in your heart for your father over it. You said no, it was all gone. Do you remember saying that?"

The Flow of Conversation

[Here is the juncture of truth, whether Andy holds up to his word or not. If he doesn't, he brands himself a liar and his word must be considered suspect.]

Andy: "Yeah."

Michelle: "Now you're saying something else. And it's causing a problem."

Andy: "The bitterness?"

Michelle: "And whether I can trust what you say or not."

Andy (reflective pause): "Maybe I am bitter. When I told you I wasn't, I didn't think I was. What else do I do that makes you think I am bitter?"

Michelle: "You take it out on me."

Andy is silent.

Michelle (ready with Scripture): "Bitterness is anti-Christian, Andy. In Ephesians 4:31 Paul says, 'Let all bitterness and wrath be put away, for the sake of the church and God and you as a priest.'"

Andy: "You're right."

Michelle: "Are you a priest or not?"

Andy: "You got me."

Michelle: "No, the Bible does. But something else. Proverbs 5:4 says the bitter one is bitter as wormwood, like it grows and gets worse. And if this means your bitterness toward your father makes you like that, I'm not safe in this relationship."

Andy (possible diversion): "Hand me the Bible over there."

Michelle (staying on track): "First, please listen. I like you very much and we have a lot of good in this relationship. We both have children to think about. But nothing is worth going against the warnings of the Bible. If it warns me to step back, I'm gonna have to do it."

Andy: "What can we do?"

Michelle's diary:

Confronted Andy reg. bitterness after fam. visits. A open to discuss, but began denying problem. After explaining, A. told me to leave. Angry. Reminded A. of earlier agreemnt to comm. problems—he tried harder.

Reminded A. of Feb. 10 conv. at Kava House—"I'm not bitter anymore" and "I'm not bitter at my father." Admitted some bitterness toward F. Read Eph. 4:31 to A. He agreed w/it, said, "You got me." A. saw bitterness, said, "What can we do?" Apologized. Agreed to get help on this. Made plans to see counselor . . ."

A person should not have difficulty seeing the advantage of the two books involved here, the Bible and Michelle's diary. They give her the authority to spiritually become Nathan and point the finger at Andy, using his own words and the truth of the Bible.

Two things are noteworthy. One, whenever a Christian man goes against either his own word or the Word of the Bible, a massive character flaw is on display for him to see. Whether he sees it or remains blind is extremely valuable feedback.

Second, when seeing his character flaw elicits some form of guilty plea, as Andy finally pled with, "What can we do?" a great thing has happened. Rejoice, the person is in the mood of repentance. It's time to call off the dogs, congratulate (or embrace) the person, and begin working on an amicable solution.

> **It is the offender's repentance which signals the dawning of a new day. Your forgiveness and his repentance must be equal.**

Before going any further, a word about the female's response to male repentance. Know that a man does a huge thing in moving his ego aside and accepting fault. The Holy Spirit is involved. The Christian response is defined in

The Flow of Conversation

Phil. 3:13, ". . . Forgetting what is behind . . ." In other words, the event is forgiven, you weigh his atonement, and move on. A genuine repentant attitude deserves your total forgiveness.[7]

If the repentance is for something severe and agonizing, the error must be turned over to God and forgiven.[8] Frequently, counseling is required to achieve this step, since the struggle to forgive may be too agonizing alone. However, it is the offender's repentance which signals the dawning of a new day. Your forgiveness and his repentance must be equal.

Last, the ultimate lesson in this example is that Andy has become aware of his bitterness and it's effect on Michelle, which he could not see before. Angel's work brought it to light. A course of correction can begin.

Conducting Your Conversations

The last thing you want is for your oath-triggering conversations to sound like an inquisition. Nor do you want to appear like an overly cautious, worry-wart personality. This is neither healthy or appealing. A good rule to go by? Whenever the conversation begins sounding like an interrogation, switch the conversation to yourself and model the transparency you are looking for. By doing this you set an example of openness, which is how you would like the conversation characterized.

General to Specific

In pursuing an issue to draw out a person's oath, it is always best to go from general to specific. In other words, rather than begin the discussion by saying, "I'd like to know what your spending habits are," it would be best to begin with something like, "Does your paycheck seem to go faster than it should, like mine does?" This opens several roads in the direction of spending habits. Another could be, "I'm the kind of person who, if I don't watch it, once I buy something I'm liable to buy something else in the next five minutes. Do you ever do that?" Chances are good that his response could then allow, "Are you able to stay within your means?" This may sound nosey, but not if you've noticed something out of kilter and want some word on it. Besides, a best-foot-forward response may come in handy when he asks you for a loan.

Sometimes you may get nothing worthy of your diary. For example, the above question might get this response: "Usually." Well constructed and direct follow-up statements can help.

"So you don't have a problem with over-spending like some people do."

If the person is still cautious you could still get, "Not usually." If that happens, try something like, "Usually to me sounds like it isn't (can be) a problem. If it was, I take you for a person who would own up to it."

If you still get a grunt or a one-word answer, file it away in your diary as "non-committal," a viable subject to be pursued at another time. If the person can open up on other topics but not spending, then spending becomes a topic worthy of your suspicion.

But chances are good you will hear a best-foot-forward response if approached early enough in the courtship. "I don't have a problem with living beyond my means," is a more likely response. This is what you are after.

Again, the purpose of pursuing his spending habits is not just to find out what they are, but also getting his word established in case you need it some day. If you should later find that he shows irresponsibility with money, you have the means (his word) to confront it, unearth the problem[9] and reveal his character.

The Flow of Conversation

Self-Disclosure

Self-disclosure is always valuable in promoting an open response. Self-disclosure is telling something about yourself, how you think, in hopes of getting the same from the other person, sort of a trade of information in which you go first. Self-disclosure lets the other person see that it is okay to have an open door discussion. As a bonus, it allows you to establish your own position and provides a standard by which to adhere.

In the following examples, try to imagine what response these self-disclosure statements would get from a suitor putting his best foot forward.

"I'm against domestic violence in all cases. How about you?"

"I've had my passion for collecting records and CDs sometimes get out of hand. Has something like that ever happened to you?"

"I don't know about you, but I don't want to be in a relationship if I can't trust the other person."

"I've never had a problem with alcohol or drugs. How about you?"

Let's take one to completion.

She: "I still struggle with my anger. If I feel myself going off, I'll just go take a walk if I feel myself getting worked up. What do you struggle with?"

He: "Not anger."

She: "No? What then? Everybody struggles with something. If you don't, you're the first person I've ever met who doesn't."

He (with Christian frankness): "Well, in the past I've had to lie my way out of a lot of situations. I don't talk like I used to, but the urge, the knack, for the quick way out is still there."

She: "How were you able to get away from it, I mean, break the habit?"
He: "Whenever I caught myself, I went back and said it right. I might even say, 'Look, what I just said wasn't right. Let me say it again. I did leave the door unlocked,' or whatever."
She: "It must have been humbling and hard. Do you still do that if you need to?"
He: "Sometimes."
She: "I want you to know that if you ever catch yourself fibbing to me and want to change it to the truth, it will always be okay. I'd rather have that."
He: "Okay."
She: "Then you will? I mean, change something you say if it isn't right?"

I ask you, what is the man going to say to this question? At this point, regarding something as important as telling the truth, the woman could lock it up completely by saying, "Every time? Have I got your word on that?" but this isn't necessary if it has been accepted that a Christian's utterances may be considered oaths. Just the fact that the person has spoken the words and you've recorded them accurately are enough.

Point number two. Don't miss the effect of this woman's acceptance on this man's admitted sin. If the Holy Spirit is alive in this man, he would sooner drive over a cliff than lie to her.

Never be punitive or form an opinion after your partner opens himself up honestly. For instance, when the above person admitted to being a liar in the past, the woman could have thought, "A liar. That's a character flaw." Of course it is. But by chipping away at it we find that the man is willing to be open about it and is fighting a great fight, both of which are character highlights.

The Flow of Conversation

Other Oath Opportunities

Don't miss the opportunity to pick up on idle chatter and develop it into a valuable journal entry. For instance, you are a passenger in his car. The radio reports that a halfback is suspended from football for hitting his wife.

"What do you think about that?" she asks.

He gives an answer that shows mild agreement.

"It sounds like you are against a man hitting his wife," she replies.

He concurs. She clarifies it until it becomes worthy of her journal.

Notice in the above example that one doesn't have to ask a question to get a response. By restating or summarizing the person's response you almost always get a further response. If he doesn't offer more, his silence then begs another statement or question. Say that instead of responding to the statement, "It sounds like you are against a man hitting his wife," he remains silent, which is a possible betrayal of his feelings. The woman could then follow up with the opposite, "Then again, maybe you aren't against it."

From here she gets either, "Oh, I am, all right" or, "Not in every case" which requires further discussion. If she gets nothing it could be even better. She could then say, "You know what? I just asked you if you were against a man hitting his wife and you ignored it." He's got to answer that.

Soften Your Questions

There is nothing wrong with feeling around for an answer on a particular point until it becomes painfully obvious what you are doing. A Christian man should have no trouble honoring your efforts. However, be careful not to be too direct with single questions. Rather than saying, "Do you have good manners?" you would do better to ask questions like these:

"What kind of manners do you think a man should have?"; "Should manners be important to us?" or, "Are manners important to you?" Instead of, "Would you hit a child for misbehavior?" soften it by saying, "What is your opinion on punishing a child for misbehavior?"

Rather than, "Do you wear good clothes to church?" try, "What do you think the Lord's opinion is on the way a person dresses for church?" Something like this not only lets you in the side door of the issue, it can reveal the person's perceived knowledge of Scripture (see Psalm 29:2). However, the softer question might not get the information you are after. "How do *you* think a person should dress going to church on Sunday morning?" should.

Perhaps the value of asking for opinions like these can be seen in the last question, "How do *you* think a person should dress going to church on Sunday morning?" Can we imagine a man or woman giving an opinion to that question and then two Sundays later go completely against it? In this way, his stated opinion, so long as it is a good one, can establish his behavior for years to come in an area which may otherwise be undefined. In this case, the man who states that appropriate dress is acceptable to God is forced to stick to his word. If not, a character-revealing confrontation is born.

Example:

"A couple weeks ago you said a person should dress respectfully for church. It doesn't matter to me, but is this what you meant?"

If his reply is testy, apologize and see if he returns the courtesy. If not, it could signal difficulty in working things out.

Whenever a person avoids an issue, feel free to bring it right back. For example, a woman says, "The Bible, particularly in the New Testament, has a lot to say about the role of a man in marriage. Do you agree with it?"

The Flow of Conversation

> Man: "It's a pretty tricky balance between men and women. Everyone has a different marriage. My dad did it one way, my uncle another. Both were pretty happy though."
> Woman: "I mean, what do *you* think about what the Bible says about the role of a man in marriage. Do you agree with it?"
> Man: "Me, I've never been married."
> Woman: "You may have never read what the Bible says about the man's role."
> Man: "Oh, I've read it."
> Woman: "Maybe you aren't in total agreement with it then."

By this time he will have to submit something or else continue to evade it, which is something you may profit from. Understanding where a man refuses to commit his word can be as valuable as to where he will.

Certainly by now, heart-wrenching as they may be, you can see the value in a person's poor responses. When these occur, accept them without debate. They may become topics worthy of further discussion down the road. Be sure to note them in your journal.

Yes and No Questions

When attempting to open up and expand conversations, you may experience some initial difficulty. This may come as the result of two errors: 1) asking one-word response-type questions with no follow-up, or 2) allowing your partner to cleverly escape issues.

An example of a question which will get a one-word answer is, "Do you like to read the Bible?" This is a question that can be answered yes or no, allowing that discussion to be ended in one word, putting the ball back in your court quickly. The same can be said for, "What is your favorite book of the

Bible?" or, "Do you think honesty is important to a relationship?" The answers to the above questions are, yes, Psalms, and yes. However, one-word response questions do not have to stop conversations as along as you have a follow-up question ready.

The person answers yes to the first question. The listener quickly adds, "What do you enjoy most about reading the Bible?" This pulls out more of an answer and sets up the commission of his word. For instance:

He: "I enjoy the peace it offers. Also, I like the history."
She: "I like the inner peace, too. What does the history do for you?"
He: "I think it shows God's hand in the affairs of men—what He honors and how He works."

Journal Entry

Todd says reading the Bible gives him a sense of peace and shows him how God works in men's lives.

This woman now has a point to raise should Todd's faith be undercut by straying from the Scriptures.

The question asking about his favorite book pulled Psalms as the short answer. "Why?" would elicit more, but a better question would be, "That's interesting. What do you get out of it?" If you wished to add a bit of self-disclosure you could say, "I enjoy that book, too. I learned a lot about prayer from Psalms. What did you get?"

When He Avoids an Issue

Topics as important as the five fundamentals in chapter seven need pinning down. Prompts such as the following can be used to do this.

(Statement) "In my opinion, honesty is something two people need to discuss and not take for granted. (Self-disclosure) I took *faith* is the SUBSTANCE! HEBREWS 11:1

FAITH TRUTHS

GALATIANS 3:11

Faith in God is my key to desiring, praying, believing, receiving and having all God has promised.
(Mark 11:22-25)

Faith comes to me by hearing God's WORD.
(Romans 10:17)

Faith speaks what it hears.
(Romans 10:8)

Faith is my promise of salvation by God's grace!
(Ephesians 2:8-9)

Faith is my gift from God!
(Ephesians 2:8)

Faith brings the unseen into the seen realm.
(Hebrews 11:1)

Faith has redeemed me from the curse of the law.
(Galatians 3:13)

Faith pleases God, and God rewards my faith.
(Hebrews 11:6)

Faith fights and wins!
(1 Timothy 6:12)

Faith in Christ Jesus has made me God's child.
(Galatians 3:26)

Faith has brought THE BLESSING of Abraham and The Spirit of promise upon me.
(Galatians 3:14)

KENNETH COPELAND MINISTRIES   FORT WORTH, TX 76192 // Contact us at 1-817-852-6000 // KCM.ORG

791697

The Flow of Conversation

honesty for granted once already and I learned a valuable lesson. (The point) How do you feel about honesty between two people in a relationship?"

It is tough to slither away from such structured questions, but masters of slithering can do it. Generally, they will try to wrest control from you if they don't like where the conversation is going. A slithering master will answer the questions he doesn't like with anything that will allow him to remain non-committal.[10] Notice that this is often done by answering a question with a question. For example:

She: "Do you think honesty is a relationship is important?"

He: "Sure."

She: "I don't think it is something that should just be taken for granted. I did that once before and got burned. What is your opinion?"

He (butting in): "Are you somebody who is trustworthy to a fault?"

She: "What do you mean by that?"

He: "That you trust even when you shouldn't."

She (not giving up control): "Maybe, but I want to talk about honesty . . . (or more pointed) but I asked you about honesty. Tell me how you feel about it between people in a relationship."

He (depersonalizing): "*Two people* in a relationship had better be honest. If *they* don't, how can *they* have any trust?"

She (staying on track, trying for a solid journal entry): "Yes, how can they?"

He: "*They* can't."

She (personalizing): "Then *for your relationship*, honesty is included?"

He: "Well, of course."

She: "To me, honesty means not just telling the truth but also sharing things that aren't known, if they will affect the relationship. Does honesty mean that to you?"

This woman is staying on this man like a glove and pressing him fairly on an issue of much importance. By seeing his attempt to redirect things away from *his* views of honesty but not taking the bait, she maintains control of the conversation.

These examples are not meant to say that you always control the conversations. Half the time you should be following the lead of the other person. But the other half you will be leading into important areas of concern. The more adroit you are in directing these conversations, the more oaths you will have for your journal. The more oaths you have, the more tools with which to examine his character, and the more you have to offer him in terms of service as a spiritual sharpening device.[11]

Any conversation has the potential to shoot off in several directions. These side roads can be fascinating, but they should not be taken until the original topic is exhausted to your diary's satisfaction. In the conversation about a man's role in marriage, the woman could have switched directions by saying, "You may have never read what the Bible says about the man's role. Why don't we read it together some time?"

This is good, but she would have lost her original purpose— to see if he agreed with the Bible's view of a man's role in marriage. Remember, only one road can be taken at a time, and it is better to travel it for a good spell before quickly jumping to another. Whenever a conversation detours to a side road from a main road, the issue changes. And, without realizing it, you may be following a detour orchestrated by someone purposely ducking a sensitive issue which needs to be explored.

The Flow of Conversation

To the above question, the man could have masterminded a detour by saying, "Oh, I've read what the Scriptures say about the man's role in marriage. But I think more fascinating reading is Revelations. The end times are what opened the door to my accepting Christ."

The woman would be making a mistake if she responded, "Really? What did it mean to you?" Tempting as it might be, she would only be following his detour signs. She should stay on the main road by saying something like, "Really? Let's talk about that sometime. But right now I'm curious about what you think of the Bible's comments on the man's role in marriage."[12]

Practice your conversational skills with a trusted friend. With this kind of practice, you will quickly pick up valuable skills in directing and maintaining control of targeted "oath-wresting" conversation from your courting companion. Ultimately, his oaths will make you more valuable as a spiritual helper and provide you with opportunities to see his character.

If the skill of directing conversations this way seems intimidating, relax. Most men spout off regularly with opinions and ideas.[13] Simply listening to what comes out will offer plenty of oaths. Example:

Fred: "Did you see the way Jim spoke to Mary? I can't believe he said that to her."

Journal Entry

Fred was upset that Jim raised his voice to Mary and insinuated she was dumb . . .

Don: "The problem with most relationships is that the people in them take each other for granted."
Confrontation: "Once, May 4th, you said, 'The

problem with relationships is that the people in them take each other for granted.' Is that what is happening when you assume my weekends are always open?"

Sam: "Even the R-rated movies are X today. If I can't find a PG movie with a decent story line, I'm not going."

Sam then rents two R-rated movies for a home date. Beth sifts his character by saying, "I thought you said you weren't going to watch any more R-rated movies." After, she doesn't argue his reaction, she merely examines it for clues to the inner Sam and logs it away for future reference, if necessary.

Chuck: "Remember that scene in the movie when he asked her how she felt about perverted sex? That was her first clue that something was wrong."

Journal Entry
February 20.
Tonight Chuck asked me, 'Remember that scene . . .'"

Endnotes

1. Job 1:7: "The LORD said to Satan, 'Where have you come from?' Satan answered the LORD, 'From roaming through the earth and going back and forth in it.'" Eph. 6:12: "For our struggle is not against flesh and blood, but against the rulers, against the authorities, against the powers of this dark world and against the spiritual forces of evil in the heavenly realms."
2. Prov. 9:8: ". . . rebuke a wise man and he will love you." Prov. 28:23: "He who rebukes a man in the end will gain more favor . . ."

The Flow of Conversation

3. Prov. 23:15-16 (reverse gender): "My son, if your heart is wise, then my heart will be glad; my inmost being will rejoice when your lips speak what is right."
4. Prov. 21:29: "A wicked man puts up a bold front . . ."
5. Prov. 18:7: "A fool's mouth is his undoing, and his lips are a snare to his soul."
6. Prov. 28:23: "He who rebukes a man will in the end gain more favor than he who has a flattering tongue."
7. Prov. 17:9: "He who covers over an offense promotes love . . ."
8. Prov. 20:22: "Do not say, 'I'll pay you back for this wrong!' Wait for the LORD, and he will deliver you."
9. Eph. 5:11: "Have nothing to do with the fruitless deeds of darkness, but rather expose them."
10. Prov. 18:13: "He who answers before listening—that is his folly and his shame."
11. Prov. 25:4: "Remove the dross from the silver, and out comes material for the silversmith." Prov. 27:17: "As iron sharpens iron, so one man sharpens another."
12. Prov. 20:5 (reverse gender): "The purposes of a man's heart are deep waters, but a man of understanding draws them out."
13. Prov. 18:6-7: "A fool's lips bring him strife . . . and invites a beating. A fool's mouth is his undoing, and his lips are a snare to his soul."

"With their tongue they speak deceit."
—*Psalm 5:9*

11

Detours

What follows is a small list of detours and side-tracking tricks you can expect to find on your quest to establish your partner's position on relevant issues. The list cannot specify every ruse a person may use to gum up the works, but it does a good job of showing the type of difficulties you may run into.

In running into the following detours, it is extremely important to note in your diary when the detour occurred and the subject matter which caused the detour to happen. This way you can plan another strategy and return to the topic later.

Evasive Tactics

1. Changing the subject

This can result from discomfort with the topic or unwillingness to commit an opinion. This person may have ideas other than that which would normally be expected.

Example:
Woman: "And while we're on the subject of your nieces, do you enjoy children?"
Man: "Oh, of course. Isn't it a beautiful morning? I haven't seen a morning like this in a month it seems. On days like this I always think of the sea."

The unrelated change of subject is an evasive tactic. In this case, it suggests steering clear of deepening the relationship with talk of fatherhood. If follow-up inquiries don't help, make a note in your diary along with a reminder to pursue the topic at a later date.

2. Vague answers and comments
The person may not know anything about the subject matter or is unsure of what you are asking.
Example:
She: "What does salvation mean to you?"
He: "More of a relationship with the Creator. We're all made by something more infinite that we can imagine, and to be aware of this, our oneness with the universe, is more rewarding than life without God."

With an answer like this, chances are good that this person is not grounded in Christian doctrine. It probably means that he has a vague, worldly view of Christianity rather than enlightenment by the Holy Spirit. Once this has been determined, be gentle. If not, you will run the risk of an inquisition and perhaps suspected judgment—a real turn-off to a person desiring but not having a Christian experience. Make a note in your diary to help him along in his faith. For the time being, step back and avoid emotional bonding until the person becomes a grounded Christian.

3. Evasiveness. Deliberate avoidance of a particular subject

The man may be anticipating the line of questioning and quickly short-circuits the process by suddenly darting away. An example would be topics relating to intimacy. The man may have a fear of talking freely about relational matters. He may also be holding back emotionally.

Example:
> She: "The Song of Solomon is a passionate book about the joy of love. Do you see it that way?"
> He: "I haven't read it."
> She: "Mind if I tell you what I know about it?"
> He: "I'd rather talk about some other book. The epistles are much more practical."

In a case like this, steering away from the Song of Solomon's romantic innuendo should be noted along with a reminder to go back to this subject in the future.

4. Hostile reactions. A sudden turn to your line of conversations characterized by hostile words or actions

Example:
> She: "To me, how people go about their job is very important."
> He: "Why is everything a person does always *very important* to you? You sound like a snob who thinks everyone has to qualify before you'll give them the time of day."

Hostile reactions are always a bad sign.[1] They should never be ignored. These uncomfortable times must be discussed in detail, regardless of the discomfort they may cause, *but usually not at the time of the hostile reaction.*[2] However, no more than a day or two should come between the incident and it's subsequent discussion, which needs scriptural backing. The time between the incident and your discussion gives the man a chance to make up honorably. If he doesn't, he has missed the chance to redeem himself with a character move.

Whoever *absorbs* the dose of hostility should apologize for their part, right or wrong, and take care to remain respectful to the hostile person.[3] There are two reasons for this. First, it is the Christian response which you are required to make. Second, as the offended person you display a powerful character model when you absorb hostility without returning it.

In your journal, note the subject matter which caused the hostile reaction. There is a hot-button in there somewhere. Consider it a trouble spot for further clarification.

5. Self-defense.[4] *A foolish defense of self provoked by the discussion*[5]

The more fragile the self-concept, the more likely one will defend himself against perceived threats.[6] Self-defense differs from hostility in that the energy in self-defense is spent protecting one's self, while hostility is lashing out. Example:

Woman: "My appearance is very important to me, from the clothes I wear to the way I keep myself, because I feel that I am a priestess of my faith. I just want to look my best. It's the witness of my appearance. Do you feel the same?

Man (irritated): "Is there something about the way I dress you don't agree with? I don't have all the money in the world to buy all the clothes I'd like to have, or all the time I'd like to spend at the health club. If you don't like the way I look, I'm sorry."

Woman: "I didn't say that."

Man: "But that's what you mean. It's not right."

Unfortunately, it happens. It betrays a fragile makeup and remedial Christian development. Mature Christians realize that self-defense is rarely, if ever, necessary. The world perceives that attack is around every corner, but the Christian chooses to believe that a more trustworthy motive is at the brother's or sister's hand. A good response is made by remaining defenseless, offering an apology if necessary.

The man in this example lost the opportunity to relate in a trusting way. Instead, he released an impression of mistrust and hyper-sensitivity, something not easily erased. By offering a simple comment like, "I try to look my best and hope that my appearance is acceptable," he would have risked nothing, showed trust and kept both his dignity intact and the conversation flowing. Generally, a Christian possesses this kind of common sense.

As for courting a defensive man, it is a lot like approaching a porcupine. Don't spend too much time on one who is routinely defensive. His self-concept needs healing. You do not want this flowing into you through marriage. It is fair to confront the defensiveness directly but this may only bring on more, bring insults, or both.[7] The only benefit is that it becomes valuable character clarification. If you're serious about dealing with it, enlist a counselor.

6. Idyllic responses

This person's conversation contains nothing but ideal responses. After listening to this person's side of the conversation, you get the impression that he lives in a different, much better world than you, and that he has attained a level of personal ease that smells unreal. He characterizes himself as someone already conformed to the Image of God, and further development is no longer necessary.

> She: "There just doesn't seem to be enough hours in the day. Just today I had a list of five things to do. Five things! I have two of them checked off. Does it ever get that way for you?"

He: "Getting through five items a day isn't a problem. It's a matter of staying focused."
She: "But don't you ever fall behind on what you want to do?"
He: "No. Whenever I feel like I'm falling behind I know that I've envisioned too much and I get back to only the things I want to do. Of course, I never compromise spiritually."
She: "You must do a lot of witnessing then, too, since you are so focused."
He: "All the time. I led a person to the Lord just yesterday. Witnessing is a big part of my worship."
She (catching on): "Are you a person who fasts regularly, too?"
He: "I fast four times a year. It keeps my weight down. Any more and I'd lose too much weight."

You get the idea. Naturally, this is the easiest person to trip up with a journal, something he needs if he plans to grow as a Christian. Some of the idealist's statements could be considered outright lies and should be written down word-for-word. Bringing this to the idealist's attention in a loving way is a godly reproof of the highest order. Just don't expect anything more than an ideal response.

7. Intellectualizing. Brain power over substance

This tactic is used to avoid an issue by confusing it with a lot of misleading words. It is closer to lying than giving a genuine answer.[8] Example:

She: "I'm glad you agree that the ability to adjust to new and different situations is valuable. How are you at adjusting?"
He: "My personal tendencies probably fall somewhere within the norm. If I were to qualify as an adjuster to

every conceivable situation of say, a marriage, I or anyone else, that person risks compromise of the basic ingredient which was catalyst to the situation in the first place—himself, or in my case, myself."

She: "It sounds like you are not a person who adjusts easily."

He: "I'm being overly facetious. But it is doubtful that we could conclude anything given the hypothetical question. Before going any further, define what you mean by 'a person who adjusts'?"

This person plays mind games to escape from committing his opinion to anything. Usually, he is unconsciously trying to dominate with mental smoke while fooling mostly himself. He hides behind words. He is posturing himself in safe, non-committal stances out of habit. Such a habit is often so grooved into the personality that reverting it back into common sense is difficult if not impossible, particularly if the person has the gift (or in this case, curse) of high intelligence. The gift of intelligence often buttresses an otherwise insecure personality, and removing it risks total collapse.[9]

Intellectualization is often used as a defensive and offensive tactic whenever it can be worked to an advantage. There is no risk, however, in confronting such a thing and explaining your difficulty in connecting with the person because of it. This may get results but don't count on it lasting. A thorough, spirit-changing experience is needed to reverse the sometimes bullying habit. Clearly, such a thing is absent in the intellectualizer.

8. *Platitudes. Allowing coined phrases to do the talking*

This person tries to hide the fact that he has no genuine thought or opinion by hiding behind safe but worn out words and phrases. Or if he does, he is fearful of expressing them.

Detours

She: "What would you like to do with your future?"
He: "My motto is, 'Easy come, easy go.'"
She: "It sounds like you take life pretty easily."
He: "Another day, another dollar. It comes, it goes. I leave work at the office around five o'clock everyday. Actually it isn't so bad. I have the weekends off and let the boss worry about day-to-day operations. Life is good."
She (leaving the topic, feeling around): "I like my job. It sounds like you enjoy yours, too."
He: "My boss is a good guy to work for. He doesn't have a doghouse. Be on time, stay 'till the end, keep the sick days to a minimum, he won't bother you."

This person will commit nothing beyond the acceptable, superficial banter of the non-thinking dolt who has no passions, no opinions and no convictions. Be careful, it leaves him free of standards of conduct. Soft confrontation is needed to let him risk personalizing a response. Praise him when it happens because he won't realize what he has done. Request more. You may be surprised by what comes out.

9. The Near-but-not commitment

These are responses which sound like they could be oaths, but they are purposely worded to leave a loophole of escape. Where some men speak clearly, others speak obscurely.
Example:
Veronica: "We've talked about children a lot, John. What kind of father do you think you would be?"
John: "I like to think that I'd be a good father. A father should be concerned with his children before himself."
Veronica: "What do you think is the right size of a family, the number of children?"
John: "Two or three children would be about right."

Notice that the man in this example has committed himself to nothing by his words. For all he has said, his desire might be to remain a bachelor. He has given comment but no personalization, nothing about himself. This is very important to the journal keeper. The journal would be in grievous error it if were to contain the following: *John said he wanted to be a good father, someone who is more concerned with his children than himself. He says he'd like two or three children.*

John said nothing of the kind. He described a good father, not himself, and his opinion of a good family size, not his own. He might not want to be part of either one. If the journal author ever confronted him on these points, he would be in his rights to say, "I never said I wanted to be a father, and I never said I wanted two or three children." He would be right because he answered the questions from a philosophical standpoint rather than a personal one. He escaped via the loophole of saying the right thing but leaving himself out of it.

Let's take that conversation back to the beginning.

Veronica: "We've talked about children a lot, John. What kind of father do you think you would be?"

John: "I do like to think that I'd be a good father. A father should be concerned with his children before himself."

Veronica: "I think you'd be a good father, too. Are you saying you'd like to be one someday?"

John: "Well, I'm not sure."

Veronica: "Why the uncertainty?"

John: "It's a hard thing to put my finger on."

Veronica: "Well, tell me your thoughts about being a father."

[John is now forced to explain his thinking concerning himself as a father.]

John: "I guess I'm uncertain if fatherhood is for me."
Veronica: "You mean you don't know if you want a family?"
John: "I guess I don't know."

Another example shows the deftness of this tactic. Sherry runs into Phil during a break in a meeting.

Sherry: "After the meeting, some of us are going over to Lydia's house to listen to music and eat dessert. Want to come along?"
Phil: "That sounds like a good idea."

Phil is a no-show. The next time Sherry sees him she asks why he wasn't there.

"I never said I was going," is Phil's reply. Sherry insists that he did. A rift comes between them. In this case, Phil is right. The event was a good idea, but that is as far as he went.

Let's take the dialogue back to the beginning so that Sherry can cover her error.

Sherry: "After the meeting, some of us are going over to Lydia's house to listen to music and eat dessert. Want to come along?"
Phil: "That sounds like a good idea."
Sherry: "You'll be going then?"

Phil is now forced to commit one way or the other.

Endnotes

1. Prov. 20:3: ". . . every fool is quick to quarrel."
2. Prov. 17:14: "Starting a quarrel is like breaching a dam; so drop the matter before a dispute breaks out." Prov. 23:9: "Do not speak to a fool, for he will scorn the wisdom of your words."

3. Prov. 15:1: "A gentle answer turns away wrath but a harsh word stirs up anger."
4. Prov. 29:20: "Do you see a man who speaks in haste? There is more hope for a fool than for him."
5. Prov. 17:27: "A man of knowledge uses words with restraint, and a man of understanding is even-tempered."
6 Prov. 28:1: "The wicked man flees though no one pursues . . ."
7. Prov. 9:7: "Whoever corrects a mocker invites insult; whoever rebukes a wicked man incurs abuse."
8. Prov. 10:19: "When words are many, sin is not absent."
9. Prov. 10:8: ". . . a chattering fool comes to ruin." Prov. 10:10: "He who winks maliciously causes grief, and a chattering fool comes to ruin." Ecc. 5:7: "Much dreaming and many words are meaningless."

"Now then, stand here, because I am going to confront you with evidence..."
—*1 Samuel 12:7*

12

Confrontation

As a relationship develops, the man and woman move from "the ideal" to "the real." To show this progression, imagine four pre-engagement stages: Entry Level, Internship, Formal Confrontation, and Final Analysis. The stages allow for increasing levels of confrontation to a man's oaths/action incongruence.

In the Entry Level and Internship, the term confrontation is too strong. You are not confronting as much as you are bringing facts of his behavior before his eyes. It is more a "behavior report" done in the spirit of love and Christian service. Remember, as a woman, you have a special sphere of influence over a man's ego. Your gentle and meek spirit challenges his maleness from the inside, where the real work needs to take place. After you present the facts, you will remain silent for the most part, then base his response against Christian standards.

The four-stage structure is intended to illustrate the

developing conversation levels between two people. Naturally, structuring human interaction is a dangerous proposition. You will see large overlaps. This shows the inexactness of the progression.

Conversation Tables

Entry Level—One to four weeks building rapport. The five foundational pillars established (chapter seven). Pursuing other subjects: work, school, family, news, personal history, spiritual matters. Building acceptance. Seeing his words and oaths design a pattern of outward character.

Basically, the entry level is a time of information gathering, when the man's best foot is forward. This doesn't mean pressing a matter to full conclusion. It is simply gathering valuable bits and pieces of data which come out of casual conversation. The entry level gives a man room to write the blueprint of his character with his own words.

A woman at this level of courtship is seeing her suitor's character emerge. She knows that she is seeing neither the true man or the finished product. She will be seeing a man who answers as much to his flesh as he does the Scriptures, but she doesn't know this yet. She may be seeing an unrefined character presenting an ideal self, one which has not experienced another Christian's sharpening tools or the work of an angel.

In getting to know someone, all foundational topics (chapter seven) are fair game with which to build rapport, as long as the person feels comfortable talking about them. Prying is not wise at this point, although no harm should come from asking about the difficulty in discussing something.

Whenever two Christians converse, the most common ground is their faith. However, it is unlikely that both would

Confrontation

be at the same level of Christian development. Who knows, the two people may be at such different stages that these initial conversations may prove to be witnessing/teaching opportunities. What is at stake in the entry phase is the cohesion of two Christians at different stages of spiritual growth. It is important to get along. This is why *conditional* acceptance is necessary, the condition being that each is a Christian.[1]

Early acceptance is crucial for several tactical reasons. Acceptance allows a man the freedom to establish who he is by what he says, which is what a woman needs to hear. Ultimately, you may choose not to be with this man on a courting basis. However, until you have tested his character, you cannot make that decision. A relationship with a good man may develop slowly. The world would say that you are giving the man enough rope to hang himself with, but let's look at it in a more proactive, Christian light. Through conversation, you are giving him the opportunity to establish the guidelines of his own behavior, on which his character will be judged.[2] Also, Christian behavior is one of fairness, of granting the benefit of doubt, and of being thorough. Fair judgment means waiting until all the facts are in. The entry level is the time to be wise like the serpent and innocent as the dove. The only guidelines are to steer clear of imminent judgment, sexual matters, or inappropriate personal matters.

During the entry level, the wise woman does not confront an issue as soon as it occurs. She waits until the matter is crystal clear, knowing that without the facts in proper alignment, confrontation can be seen as meddlesome and judgmental. She does not "jump" the man's words. If the man experiences being tied up in knots with his own words too early, he may become cautious in opening up again. This is why the confrontations at this stage, if any, are soft and nonaccusatory.

The Toothless Confrontation

The only confrontation eligible at the entry level stage is one which has no teeth.[3] These "toothless confrontations" are light-air things which often contain humor. Rather than, "You once said that swearing wasn't necessary and that you stopped doing it when you were saved. I've heard you swear three times in the past two days. What is it, do you swear or don't you?" take the teeth out of it. Offer instead, "Don't I remember you once saying you didn't like to swear? . . . do you know you swore twice the other day? Just thought I'd mention it."

With good rapport and a sensitive spirit, these toothless confrontations (TCs) can be as effective as a formal confrontation with facts. TCs do not press for a resolution. The woman uses one and then steps back to see the reaction. Good or bad, the reaction goes unchallenged.

> He: "Dinner over at my mother's. Why tonight? I can think of a million things I'd rather do than that."
> She: "You can? I took you for a guy who lived by the Ten Commandments. What is that one about honoring your mother and father?"

Since it involves his word, each use of a TC should get a favorable response. A sharp retort or defensive response to a TC would wave a red flag.

> She: "Somebody ought to do what to that little poodle? I could have sworn on a Bible that you told me you liked animals."

> Heather: "That sounds like gossip to me."
> Dan: "Well, yeah, it is."

Confrontation

> Heather: "I thought you were the guy who doesn't bother with it."

TCs display a man's character in baby steps. A man will generally react only two ways. He can admit wrongdoing or he can defend his actions. Ideally, the Christian sees his wrong and escapes via repentance. If he doesn't, he will defend himself with rationalization, excessive words, tortured logic or any other means of defense. In this case, he will be giving you a preview of what you can expect when you really confront him.

Repentance to TCs should be easy, considering how lightly the approach works on the male ego. The woman should be very interested in his response. If no acknowledgment of error or change of behavior comes forth when the approach is light, can any more be expected from a stronger confrontation?

Any woman who is intimidated by confronting a man can probably get a good read on a man's character on TCs alone. Using them will raise her ability to confront as she goes along. A TC plus Scripture increases to a "gentle" confrontation. Example:

> She: "Don't I remember you once saying you didn't like to swear?. . . do you know you swore twice the other day? Just thought I'd mention it."
> He: "Oh that. Guess I'll keep my swearing to myself."
> [Adding Scripture escalates the TC to a gentle confrontation.]
> She: "Proverbs 4:24 says, 'Put away perversity from your mouth, keep corrupt talk far from your lips.' James 5:12 says it even clearer, 'Above all, do not swear . . .'"

Internship—Four to sixteen weeks exchanging feelings, discussing spiritual matters, establishing his word, oath and opinion on basic matters. Silently comparing words to actions. Probing for clarification of words and oaths. "Gentle" confrontations.

Couples moving past an entry level enter something more involved. This could be called an internship, something like a mock version of an engagement period. The best-foot-forward period is winding down and character is being laid bare. This deeper level of involvement allows for more directed conversation, which brings out more oaths defining the person's character.

One thing a woman entering the internship phase should be concerned with is time and emotional involvement. You do not want to throw your time and emotions into a dead-end relationship. This man may not be the person God has in mind for you. This is not a reason to rush anything, just a concern of which to be aware.

To limit the gamble of time, you are actually hoping for word-action discrepancies which can be confronted so that character matters can be cleared up. You may have a confrontation in the works but are wisely holding off until all the facts are in. With all the facts, a case can be presented, perhaps involving several discrepancies. However, the man under analysis may not have had enough time to knit the garment of his character and show it to you yet. Once he does, soft but effective confrontation can move the relationship to a higher level.

Complete journal entries are very important in this stage. Entries are best made within the day so that accuracy is maintained. Reviewing the entries is essential to planning your confrontations. By reviewing, the journalist will spot conversational gaps which need filling in. Accurate quotes following the words "He said" are crucial.

For instance, a journal says, *Jerry told me about his dog Patches when he was growing up.* He said *he likes animals, and that his childhood wouldn't have been the same without Patches. I hope he feels the same way about cats, because of what Tabby was to me.*

This journalist may realize that some men like dogs but don't like cats. She makes a note to tell Jerry about Tabby and ask him what he thinks about cats, and what he would do if his wife wanted one. If he is negative on cats, she may or may not debate the cat issue with him. She may wish to combine the issue with another one which slants the relationship in his direction for a more thorough case. By showing him that it tends to be *his* choice of movies, *his* schedule they work around, and now *his* choice of pets, she may get her wish after all. If not, she should hit the brakes.

Remember, good men tend to be paper tigers with their women, because their comfort and happiness are important. When you find one that isn't, leave.

Gentle Confrontations

The gentle confrontation is exercised when the woman has accumulated all the data she needs to present a case of crooked oath-behavior, but chooses to do so in a friendly, informal, unofficial manner. It differs from the toothless confrontation in that she will back up her observations with as much data (journal entries, times, dates, observations, related breaches) as necessary, but she will present it in a light-hearted, completely non-threatening way. It might sound something like this:

She: "I couldn't help but notice the other day that you were late picking me up. I wonder if you noticed, too."
He: "I thought I apologized for that."

She: "Well, you did. And I accepted it. It's not that you were late, it's the pattern of it."
He: "What do you mean?"
She: "We were about ten minutes late to church last Sunday. I don't mean to nit-pick, but you asked what I meant. You've been late four out of the last six dates we've had."
He (lip-service): "Shame on me. I'll do better."
She: "I think your mother would appreciate it, too."
He: "What do you mean?"
She: "I noticed you were late going there, too. I wouldn't be making anything out of it if you hadn't told me that a Christian should be punctual. And that it seems like you're slipping."
He: "When did I say that?"
She: "On our second date, when you were late picking me up."
He: "Oh."
She: "I'm just bringing it up because you're the one who said it was important for a Christian man to be on time, and I agree with you."
He: "I said that?"
She: "Don't you remember? We were on our way to Sylvia's house, after the Thanksgiving play. You said a Christian should be on time. I said, 'Do you mean punctual?' and you said, 'what does punctual mean?' Remember?"
He: "I should have said, ah-hem, that he's punctual most of the time."
She: "So now you want to change your word on that?"

Having made her point, the woman can now step back and look for action. If it is forthcoming, she has a man she can work with. If he is full of excuses, she has a problem.

Confrontation

Furthermore, if the woman wants to, she has a right to confront *his word* about punctuality, since he is now trying to change it.

She has also left a very poignant question in the air, "So now you want to change your word on that?" Every man, not just this one, realizes what is at stake when his word is brought into question. Of course, her own word must be intact lest she leave herself open to charges of hypocrisy.

> *Remember, good men tend to be paper tigers with their women, because their comfort and happiness are important. When you find one that isn't, leave.*

A man's response to confrontation may be to confront right back. This is a poor response on his part, but it gives the woman the opportunity to model crisp acknowledgment and repentance. The privilege to confront is best earned by unreproachable behavior. This is another principal reason for the Phase I six-month to one-year period in which you are pursuing God and fitting into His will. In doing so you became much more innocent and unimpeachable.[4]

Complete character assessment requires many confrontations at different stages of the relationship. Only after several confrontations can a man's character shine through. As a smooth way of introducing confrontation in the relationship, it can be done in stages—in the entry level, toothless; gentle in the internship level, and formal confrontations in the final stages.

Killer One-liners

When you meet hard resistance to a fact-filled confrontation of any kind, or an impenetrable line of rationalization, it is time to wrap it up with a killer one-liner like:

"So you want to change your mind on that now?"
"Are you changing your word on that?"

"I remember you telling me ____ and now you are saying ____."

"I'm disappointed that your word is so easily changed."

"I thought men kept their word when they gave it."

"I took you for a person who spoke his word."

"I think I misjudged you. When you said your word was reliable, I believed it."

Lines like these will not sit well with any man's conscience. Because they brand his word as changing and untrustworthy, they go right into his bones. They are a last-ditch effort on your part to allow him to see the error of his ways. One of two reactions to these one-liners is likely. He will either rationalize/deny or see his error. A man who will rationalize his word waves the ultimate red flag.

Formal Confrontation—Twelve to twenty-four weeks testing his words and oaths in basic matters with various forms of confrontation, analyzing the reactions to the confrontations, testing previously sidestepped and incomplete opinions and oaths.

Only if a woman wants to further a relationship does gentle confrontation transform into formal confrontation. As emphasized before, confrontations are done primarily for a glimpse into the character, secondarily for behavior change. As for seeing character, when a woman uses formal confrontation she trades in her reading glasses for a magnifying glass.

Formal confrontations have an air of importance. Whereas toothless confrontations are a type of friendly feedback with little or no follow-up, and gentle confrontations leave an open door of escape, formal confrontations are ones which use all

Confrontation

the facts at hand and press for a Christian resolution. Responses which indicate repentance are passing grades. Stubbornness, rationalizations and defensiveness, particularly with a raised voice, are always failing grades.

Formal confrontations must take place only in a mature relationship.[5] They offer the set of facts which directly contradict the man's word. The facts are thoroughly backed up with circumstances surrounding his word and the failure of his actions to follow his word. Example: Carol decides to confront Mark, a man she has been seeing exclusively for eight months, over his relationship with her children.

> Carol: "I'm glad you were able to come over early tonight, Mark. I need to discuss something with you."
> Mark: "What is it?"
> Carol (turning the television off): "Sit down."
> [Mark sits down wondering what is on Carol's mind. She has spoken with him before like this, and it usually means something about their relationship. He is thinking, what could be wrong now?]
> Carol: "I want to thank you for all the things you have done in this relationship, the good times, the kindness, the money you've spent. I hope it keeps getting better."
> Mark: "Go ahead. What's the matter?"
> Carol: "With so much good, I hate to bring this up, but I must. It's David and Barbara (her children) and you. You're not getting along."
> Mark: "Have they said something?"
> Carol: "No. It's just there. I'm their mother. I feel it and so do you."
> Mark: "I know. They just don't like me. They like their dad and I don't blame them for that. They chose sides and took his. I'm the odd guy out. I understand."

Carol: "No, it's not you *or* him. It can be both of you."
Mark: "I tried real hard in the beginning, you know that. Nothing worked. They don't respect me, they never will. They take the fact that they don't have their dad out on me. I don't have to be their doormat."
Carol: "We all have to get along, or we'll be . . ."
Mark: "They are trying to split us up and get you back with their dad. And you're caught in the middle."
Carol: "No, they won't do that. I won't let them. Mark, I have to ask you to keep trying with them. Don't give up."
Mark: "It's not much use, Carol. I know that the divorce has hurt them, but they don't respect anybody."
Carol: "There is a way. We are Christians."
Mark: "I just ignore it. I can't let it get under my skin."
Carol: "You can't ignore it and court their mother. It won't work. By ignoring them, you're giving back evil for evil. That's not how a Christian acts."
[Mark starts to talk, then stops.]
Carol: "Once I asked you what you could do in a situation like this one, and you had plenty of ideas. One was never stop trying, that love would win them over."
Mark: "I guess I was wrong."
Carol: "No, you didn't give me a guess. You told me what you could do. You said, 'Keep trying. Love will win them over.' Are you going back on that now?"
Mark: "I haven't quit."
Carol: "You just said, 'I ignore it.' Which is it, Mark? Have you quit or do you keep trying?"
[Mark stays quiet. He's been through these talks before, and he's learned not to debate Carol's truth.]
Carol: "Does a Christian man quit something where love is the answer?"

Carol brings forth the ideas Mark had in the

Confrontation

beginning of the courtship—teach David to shoot a rifle, take him rabbit hunting, just the two of them.
Carol: "And you said you'd keep it balanced. Barbara would get equal time, too. My children are Christians, aren't they? They may not act like it sometimes, but they are. Are they not your brother and sister in the Lord, Mark? Even messed up like they are?"
Mark: "Yes. They are."
Carol: "Then I am going to throw this at you. 1 John 4:20: 'If someone says, I love God and hates his brother, he is a liar . . .'"
Mark: "I don't hate your children."
Carol: "I know that. But you're not showing them love, either. You're ignoring them because it's easy. You know that being Christian is not quitting in a case like this. It is winning them over, you said so yourself."
Mark: "They . . . make it so difficult."
Carol: "I think they are seeing a Christian man avoid Christian children and it causes them to stumble."
[Mark tries to think of a way out but has nothing.]
Carol (taking her Bible): "Luke 17:2: 'It would be better for him to be thrown into the sea with a millstone tied around his neck than for him to cause one of these little [children] to sin. So . . . watch . . . yourselves.' I'm going to ask you to love them like Jesus loves you. And to keep trying, like Paul might, like you once said you would. And if there is anything you need me to do, just tell me. Will you do it?"

Only after a man has responded well to several TCs and gentle confrontations should the formal confrontation be used. They will depend on journal evidence for their teeth. You, the confronter, are ready for the defensive tactics a man may try.

You are prepared to stay on track until his chance for repentance has passed, knowing that if repentance is not forthcoming, you must emotionally distance yourself into safer territory. You must do this because of the character blemishes it reveals, and to provide the motivation a man sometimes needs to correct himself.

Such a tactic as distancing yourself carries utmost responsibility for the woman. It cannot be done flippantly, or used as a tool to manipulate. To help you decide if stepping back is necessary, be sure that your formal confrontations involve behavior in opposition to Scripture. If Scripture is not violated, your confrontation is most likely in error. Confrontations which are not in alignment with Scripture are usually an effort at manipulation.

For an example of an effective formal confrontation with facts and oaths, read the persistence of Delilah in Judges 16:16-17. However, because Delilah's confrontation does not contest scriptural behavior, it is an act of manipulation.

Once your case is stated, your task is to sit back, keep your mouth shut, and listen.[6] During the man's reply, his character will be laid bare. Examine it carefully.[7] Next, look for follow-up behavior.

A number of formal confrontations must be made prior to an engagement period to effectively reveal character and test for repentance. However, they should not be used until the internship period is passed successfully.

Confrontation and the Male Ego

What kind of effect does confrontation have on the male ego?

A man is very fearful of "losing face" to a woman because he feels it damages his place in the relationship and his ability to lead, to be a man. When used as a threat, any confrontation will backfire.[8] If he feels "strong-armed" by threatening, tactless confrontation, his ego will firm and make repentance difficult. On the other hand, if the confrontation uses facts of his behavior tactfully, acknowledgment of wrong and repentance is a much easier response for him to make.

The woman who understands this, and who wants a satisfying marriage, leaves her man's ego intact during necessary confrontation. The wise woman goes a step further. She nourishes his ego, knowing this will return to her his best. Once she establishes her lifeline to his ego, she becomes necessary and by doing so gains security. Being the nourishment for his ego, this woman is able to confront without challenge.

A Christian male should realize the value of a female's labor in holding him to his word. If he doesn't realize this value, the female has the right to question his commitment to Christ, as well as the health of his ego.

Final Analysis—Twenty-four to fifty-two weeks. Sorting thorough behavior deficiencies, weekly meetings with formal confrontations, marital plans discussed, prying into matters of concern where appropriate, pursuing counseling in problematic areas.

The relationship enters a period of final analysis after the man has successfully passed necessary formal confrontations. Rapport should have developed so that polite confrontations are a welcomed interaction which is given and received in the spirit of love. By this time, confrontation should be accepted as a means of deepening the couple's commitment to each other.

Continual information gathering is always in progress, and here a portion of the conversations delve into the deeper issues like the use of alcohol, drugs or sexuality. Final grading of character and behavioral deficiencies should be taking place.

Discussions on emotional commitment, spiritual alignment, family planning and child rearing are examples of heavier items which can also be discussed. If a man has been divorced, or had previous broken relationships, it is important to know why the relationships ended, and if necessary change has been apparent. Have healing adjustments taken place? Are the troublesome behaviors realized and eliminated from this relationship? These discussions can take place in air-tight, formal discussions or in informal meetings. In these, both people share the floor and are free to express their wants, needs and desires, and with them their oaths.

Informal meetings can and should take place at any time a couple wishes to make them. They differ from weekly scheduled meetings in the content discussed and in the *ad hoc* scheduling. As the relationship develops, they provide excellent atmosphere for confrontations which require more bite than the TCs.

Weekly Meetings

Weekly meetings occur when a couple sets aside everything to discuss specific aspects of their relationship. This means the television is off, children are not present, the phone is taken off the hook (sounding the gavel) and politeness rules. The Bible is within easy reach. Each person is granted as much "floor time" as necessary. There is a set time each week, for example, Sunday, 7:00 P.M., with a minimum time limit of perhaps fifteen minutes with a flexible maximum. The meeting may or may not hold confrontations.

One item up for business in weekly meetings is the man's (or woman's) new behavior gained from previous confrontations. If an earlier confrontation was about his foul mouth, how is his current speech? If a confrontation was about his care of the children, how is it now? If the confrontation involved his temper, how is he doing now? Scriptural references are applicable.

This is also the time when marriage plans, childrearing, social expectations, sexuality and financial matters are exhumed. At the latest, these should take place prior to the engagement.

You would do well to see these meetings as the inspection of contractual agreements between partners in a business relationship. This might sound unromantic, but when these meetings are conducted with love and concern they can become some of the most romantic moments in a relationship, drawing the couple closer together. If they are seen to drive the couple further apart, a red flag is waving.

Weekly meetings can also serve as a platform of mutual reproof. Permission is granted by each partner to confront the other in matters of spiritual or personal behavior. This contains the reproof, which is limited by time. Adhering to these scheduled meetings is a sure-fire remedy to avoid the perils of Proverbs 19:13.[9]

Both weekly and informal meetings round out the character analysis of the man under study and set the stage for engagement. They monitor a man's ability to repent, see and listen, make adjustments, negotiate fairly or unfairly, live up to his word, embark on an improved path, as well as his ability to understand your needs.

It should also be realized that unless a man responds favorably to confrontation in the early stages of a relationship, there is little point in holding weekly or informal meetings. Without being receptive to Christian confrontation, a man would be unable to function within such a meeting. This would severely limit the communication required for a successful marriage.

Heaven on earth is when a woman finds herself in a marriage where weekly meetings are welcome and confrontation consists only of the toothless and gentle variety. Hell is when she finds herself emotionally attached to a man who cannot pass the test of fact-filled confrontation.

Imagine the couple who, without so much as looking into each other's eyes and discussing their union, will recite vows without even knowing if their spouse has the ability to *listen*, to process feedback to a Christian solution, in addition to being in the dark about the capabilities of his or her character. Vows to God are then broken as the marriage deteriorates. This is an extremely hazardous route to both a successful marriage and a clean relationship with God.

Confrontations and weekly meetings eliminate the blind beginning and reduce the risk of broken vows.

Late Term Detachment

One of the most difficult things to do in a mature relationship is to pull away when necessary, particularly when a lot of time, energy and emotions have been spent. However, scriptural validation can give bones to this difficult move. When a man remains in violation of scriptural behavior after fair confrontation, your withdrawal is scripturally called for and justified.[10]

Endnotes

1. 2 Cor. 6:14: "Do not be yoked together with unbelievers . . ."
2. Ezek. 36:19: ". . . I [God] judged them according to their conduct and their actions."
3. Prov. 25:15: ". . . a gentle tongue can break a bone."
4. 1 Tim. 4:12: "Don't let anyone look down on you . . . set an example for the believers in speech, in life, in love, in faith, and in purity."

Confrontation

5. Prov. 27:5: "Better is open rebuke than hidden love."
6. Job 12:11: "Does not the ear test words as the tongue tastes food?"
7. 1 Th. 5:21: "Test everything. Hold on to the good."
8. 1 Tim. 5:1: "Do not rebuke an older man harshly. . ."
9. Prov. 19:13 (both genders): ". . . a quarrelsome wife is like a constant dripping."
10. Titus 3:10: "Warn a divisive person once, and then warn him a second time. After that, have nothing to do with him."

Phase IV:

An Inward Look

Courting Conduct

A New Start

Single Life

> *"The ordinances of the Lord are sure and altogether righteous . . . By keeping them is your servant warned; in keeping them there is great reward."*
> —Psalm 9:9-11

13

Courting Conduct

The length of a courtship can be determined by a single factor. Simply, it should be long enough to have sifted the character of your man, long enough to erase the doubts every woman should have when entering a long-term relationship.[1] It is not surprising that most divorces are caused by courtships which were either too short or too deficient in sifting the character of the people involved.

A relationship must last long enough for the woman to see the evidence of genuine love, kindness and repentance, long enough for her to see concrete movement in the direction of conforming to the Image, long enough for her to see permanence of repentant behavior brought about by confrontation. How long is this? Long enough for the act to wear thin and the real person to take the stage—long enough for wisdom to declare, "This is who he is."

Courting Conduct

Behavior runs in deep channels that were cut during early childhood, and it is very difficult to alter them. Courtship, after the glamour wears off, is a fairly good preview of what your married life will be like. If you aren't able to de-program the man during courtship, you certainly won't after marriage, when your leverage as a single woman is converted to his authority. Therefore, if you can't live with a characteristic that shows up during courtship, it may plague you for the rest of your life if you marry into it.

For example, Todd has shown Sue a character with a lot of fleshy baggage. To pinpoint this baggage, Sue sifts Todd through the Proverbs checklists in chapter three. As a result, she has decided to apply the brakes. In explaining to Todd she says, "Several Proverbs are warning me about our relationship." She presents a case of nine proverbs describing his behavior. "These have to be cleared up before we go on…"

Todd now is forced to redeem himself in Sue's eyes or lose the relationship. If he can do this, by making oaths and living up to them, he could save their relationship. For this couple, courting conduct becomes focused on character change.

One of the best possible predictors of marital success is when each partner becomes a better person *and* a better Christian during the courtship period. The opposite is also true. A "guesstimate" of time needed to sift character would be eight to twenty-four months, depending on the age, clarity of assessment, and Christian development of the couple. At some point however, after the oath-gathering and confrontation have been applied, a lengthy courtship can bring diminishing returns, as disappointment makes the heart grow weak.[2] This in mind, the sifting period should trace a jagged, ascending time line leading to marriage, rather than one which weaves a horizontal direction but makes no progress.

Dating Non-believers

If a man does not know Christ but wants a relationship with you, the guidelines are clear. He doesn't stand a chance until he has a personal relationship with the living God. Offer your testimony as a way of explanation. No matter what his reaction may be, his spirit to compete will cause him to consider your words. Your testimony will either draw him near or drive him away. Again, more angel's work as a single woman.

Single women have been given a tremendous influence to point men toward Jesus. Their words ring in a man's ears for a long time. When you capture that vision, being a single will become fun. No longer will you need to put up a shield and spend time weeding out the undesirables before they have a conversation with you. Just assume that any man who wants to have a conversation with you will quickly hear about Jesus Christ via your testimony. You don't have to formally date them to tell about Jesus. By opening yourself to conversation this way, you may discover a man God has been directing your way.

Gauging Carnality

A true Christian man will have his flesh slain by the Holy Spirit[3] and be subjected to a renewed mind.[4] Through this operation, his flesh loses its place as governor of his behavior. However, like embers that quickly stoke a flame, his carnality still burns.

Every man will have some carnality because he is made of flesh and has a sinful nature. But carnality comes in different degrees. Some men have flesh that seems to be predisposed to a lot of personal corruption. If they have come to the Lord late in life, they may have spent years grooving powerful, fleshy behaviors that now hound them. Others' carnality is more tranquil, given to relatively mild struggles. A woman should always measure the level of remaining carnality in a man before cleaving to it.

Some believers are forced to wage a daily battle against their fleshy desires. Some Christians' hearts are hardened by sin[5] and they maintain a passive battle against God. God has no choice but to apply further pressure in hopes of breaking through. This will mean a lot of anguish for the wife.

A godly man leads by his conscience. But many men have had their consciences so seared by sin that they can no longer distinguish the boundaries between sin and righteousness. Unless they are reborn, they have lost their means to lead you spiritually.

Through well-rounded assessment, you should be able to gauge your partner's carnality and place it on a scale like the one below.

|—————————|—————————|—————————|—————————|—————————|
Unsaved   Carnal Christian   Saved   Born Again   Righteous

A woman would be unwise to pair off into a relationship with anyone to the left of "Saved." If a man is not following Christ in all ways, attending church and following the Scriptures, he cannot lead effectively. Submitting to an ineffective leader is a sorry life for a Christian woman. If a man's heart is not right, he becomes an ugly person all too quickly. Submitting to this kind of ugly person can be hell on earth.

A Christian woman may have become involved with someone who at first appeared to be saved, but further sifting revealed a carnal Christian. She should exercise her wisdom by leaving the relationship, carefully explaining her position softly but clearly. Then she must make a strong stand.

The problem with a carnal man is that he operates on the elementary principles of his ego. His competitive nature will seek out and dominate a woman's cooperative/competitive nature, guaranteeing unholy battles. He will fit her conveniently into the periphery, his selfish schemes. She won't be #1. His security will take precedence over hers. Breaking her heart, or God's, will not register to him. Righteous behavior which would cancel out all of this is absent.

Respect means to show reverential regard and treat with honor. Christian women would have a hard time respecting a carnal man this way. What a woman should always be looking for is the Christian whose indwelling Christ is moving him inch by inch into a righteous man, one who doesn't resist the painful tugging toward righteousness. It is the *direction* and *momentum* of progress which is key.

What if a woman finds a man to the left of center but growing and moving to the right? Often, progress like this is more important than placement because who knows how far it will go? In a short time, a carnal Christian with sincere progress can pass a stale, backsliding, born-again believer as far as a disciple of Christ and a viable lifetime partner are concerned. If this is the case, why not set standards before entering the courtship? Baptism, regular church attendance, meetings with a pastor, Bible study, Christian friends and committing his life to Christ publicly are all good moves which may allow a wise, compassionate woman to hold her ground. If you choose to consider (not date) a carnal Christian, your only choice is to hold him accountable to Christian standards.

Sexual Involvement

What counts most to the woman intent on choosing the right partner is to maintain a clear head.[6] Clear thinking means using the brain, not the heart, as the organ of judgment.[7] As the center of all flesh, the heart interferes with intelligent decision making. It thrives on fleshy stimulation—physical contact and the swoon of romance. It is empowered by sexual sin. For this reason, sound judgment is impossible when mixed with out-of-marriage sexual involvement or when the romantic aspect is out of proportion with reality.

A woman will be tempted to go to great lengths sexually if she feels it will strengthen her relationship. This is fleshy reasoning. If she gets sexually involved for this reason, she will begin a sequence which actually weakens her chances of building a strong relationship.[8]

Ray Mossholder, wise author, lecturer, and singles pastor, uses a brilliant metaphor for this problem. He calls it the "octopus effect." When threatened, the octopus releases a dense cloud of black ink to confuse its predators. Mossholder sees the same kind of cloud being released into the judgment of the single man or woman *after the first kiss!* Mossholder's wise, albeit conservative, approach suggests that much, if not all, of the character assessment be completed before the meeting of lips.

Mossholder's view has much to say about the clearness of thinking during the assessment period, which may last over a year in hard-to-read people. The problem is, how does a couple hold off from the temptation to kiss, pet or more?

Abstinence is a matter of covenant backed by resolve. A woman must realize that her flesh (or a man, his) has a life of its own, independent of her spirit. It uses every device and psychological ploy at its disposal to sway the intellect. By these ploys, the flesh rules the unregenerate person. The unmarried Christian woman displays wisdom and maturity when her spirit overrules her flesh *and her partner's flesh.*

> *Sex, when unleashed outside of marriage, is an extremely destructive force. It hands the devil a sledgehammer with which he can pound our hearts with sin until they are hard as stone. Our consciences become seared so that it no longer halts at sin. He pounds our purity until our covenant no longer exists, and our self-esteem until we are our own worst enemy.*

Kissing, petting, and sexual intercourse are so pleasurable that, once begun, the flesh will use any trick to keep it going. The flesh becomes like the junkie who will lie, steal, sell her body and risk her life to obtain drugs. In a similar way, the penalty for getting strung out on sinful physical contact is rationalization, denial, repression, blindness and eventually a stupor-like dullness that permeates all decision making. The lurch into sexual sin cancels out a person's wisdom, understanding, conviction, sound judgment and God's blessings. In Mossholder's view, the octopus effect takes over. Once the unmarried couple enters into petting, they risk entering into the law of diminishing returns. At this point, all clear-thinking vanishes. In such darkness, the person is often reduced to the equivalent thinking of a loaf of bread,[9] losing the ability to sift clearly.

Good relationships often die from a string of dumb mistakes. When they are over, people say, "How could I have done that?"; "How could I have behaved that way?"; "How could I have said such a thing?" The answer is poor judgment caused by sexual sin. This is another facet of Mossholder's octopus effect. (To reverse the octopus effect, see 2 Corinthians 3:16.)

The woman who allows herself to experiment with sex in the dating scene risks her chaste state, her judgment, and her covenant (correct relationship with God). If the relationship sours, she takes on scarring, baggage and a hardened heart. Each round of physical sex in a dead-end relationship inches her closer to the adulteress' attitude.[10]

The Curse of Premarital Sex

Premarital sex brings about its own curse via the octopus effect. In addition, premarital sex blocks God's blessing and involvement[11] for who knows how long and offers a foothold to the adversary. In the environment of sin, Satan is always given a sound hearing. All tolled, these hindrances create a network of all-out espionage against the Christian couple. In a word, a curse.

A curse is one way of stating it. It comes down to this: sex, when unleashed outside of marriage, is an extremely destructive force. It hands the devil a sledgehammer with which he can pound our hearts with sin until they are hard as stone. Our conscience becomes seared so that it no longer halts at sin. He pounds our purity until our covenant no longer exists, and our self-esteem until we are our own worst enemy. Any man who allows this to take place is a poor steward of a woman's gift of love. The woman who allows it seals her own fate as an adulteress.

The wise woman realizes that everything she does in courting will be judged as having been done before. If that involves sex, then Satan is given the opportunity to counsel each spouse on how unchaste the other is, how morally weak and how his or her previous lovers were much more adequate. Sex becomes a bad memory rather than a beautiful thing. The curse is set in motion.

How you handle this situation is a good length of your Christian walk. The best defense is to "know thy enemy." The enemy wants you blind with sexual involvement. The wise woman plays other cards. She knows that a chaste and modest spirit is more powerful than sexual ability. She knows it is something pure in her heart that actually affects a man.[12]

And of course, the clear thinking woman knows this—
Anything obtained instantly,
at little or no cost . . .
is soon discarded.

10 Ways to Handle Sexual Temptation

1. Run, be a coward, flee. (Genesis 39:12)
2. Don't put yourself in a position to test your resistance. (Proverbs 21:16)
3. Be accountable to a Godly person of the same sex. (Proverbs 27:9)
4. Be on guard at all times. (Proverbs 12:26)
5. Determine to live a scripturally pure life today. (James 4:8, Leviticus 20:7)
6. Realize that sexual sin assaults the Lordship of Jesus Christ.
7. Recognize the consequences of sexual sin in Proverbs 6:26 and 6:32.
8. Think about your children or yet-to-be-born children. Sexual sin can bring a curse upon the next generation. (Jeremiah 2:9)
9. Get a new definition of success.
10. Get a new definition of manhood or womanhood. (Proverbs 22:1)

Endnotes

1. 1 Tim. 5:24: "The sins of some men are obvious . . . the sins of others trail behind them."
2. Prov. 13:12: "Hope deferred makes the heart sick, but a longing fulfilled is a tree of life." Prov. 13: 19: "A longing fulfilled is sweet to the soul . . ."
3. Rom. 8:2-4, Gal. 5:24.
4. Rom. 12:2: ". . . be transformed by the renewing of your mind . . ."
5. Jer. 16:12: ". . . each of you is following the stubbornness of his evil heart instead of obeying me." Ps. 73:21-22: "When my heart was grieved and my spirit embittered, I was senseless and ignorant; I was a brute beast before you."
6. 1 Pet. 5:8: "Be self-controlled and alert. Your enemy the devil prowls around like a roaring lion looking for someone to devour."
7. Prov. 28:26: "He who trusts in his own heart is a fool." (NASV)
8. Prov. 19:22: "What a man desires is unfailing love . . ."
9. Ps. 38. Prov. 6:26: ". . . for the prostitute reduces you to a loaf of bread."
10. Prov. 4:23: "Above all else, guard your heart, for it is the wellspring of life."
11. Isa. 59:2: "But your iniquities have separated you from your God; your sins have hidden his face from you, so that he will not hear."
12. Prov. 19:22: "What a man desires is unfailing love . . ."

> ". . . what counts is
> the new creation."
> —Galatians 6:15

14

The New Start

In the Garden of Eden, Adam and Eve were given only one unbreakable rule, and they managed to break it. Eve recites it in Genesis 2:3:

> *From the fruit of the trees of the garden we may eat, but from the fruit of the tree which is in the middle of the garden, God has said, 'You shall not eat from it or touch it lest you die.' (Gen. 2:3 NASV)*

YOU will have only one hard and fast, unbreakable rule regarding your courting conversations, and if you break it you can expect similar consequences. That rule is:

> *Of all the topics and issues two unmarried (or married) people may discuss you may discuss, but the topic of previous sexual partners or history you shall not discuss lest the relationship die.*

The New Start

The reasoning? Same as in the Garden. You will be like God, knowing everything, but unlike God you won't be able to handle it.

Chad and Marie felt they'd died and gone to heaven. Both were in their thirties and divorced, with four children between them. After a whirlwind courtship they fell in love. Both agreed that if only they had been their first partners, neither would be divorced. Soon, however, the idyllic landscape became contaminated. As it turned out, Chad and Marie conversed a little too well. In the effort to avoid the mistakes which led to their divorces, they got the worldly notion that the past should be exhumed and examined. Thus they became amateur psychologists, sifting detail after detail of their divorces for kernels of truth. Without realizing it, their most animated topics became the offenses brought about by their previous spouses. At first Chad was bolstered by these, seeing ways in which he could become better qualified to head Marie's household. Marie also saw value in them, getting valuable information with which to harmonize their lives. Both wanted complete resurrection from the divorces in the eyes of God, their families and themselves. They left no stone unturned.

However, discussing the past, reviewing the calamities and assigning blame to the ex-spouses gained a foothold. In time, Marie began sensing an unfair line of criticism aimed at Chad's ex-wife, which characterized Chad as faultless and his ex-wife as fault filled. Marie brought this up one day. Chad saw her point and tried to balance the scales in one fell swoop. He said, off-handedly, "Well, she was pretty good in bed."

This comment was not wisdom-laden. It was a typical mistake made by a Christian man involved in a premarital sexual stupor, working with the intelligence of a loaf of bread.[1]

Marie's insecurity grabbed hold of the statement. Not wanting to appear like she was in any way inadequate, nor to convey the impression that lack of sexual ability on her part had been a problem, one day she inferred that her ex-husband was very meticulous in his love-making and quite satisfied. She even added, "We were never bored in bed." It was a self-defending reply, made by a woman with wisdom riddled by sexual sin.[2]

These stinging indiscretions did nothing but magnify their human insecurities. With these rather innocent, self-serving statements, both Chad and Marie acquired larger-than-life rivals, ghosts which would forever haunt them. After they married, each time Chad or Marie was exposed to the other's ex, either by phone or in person (and there was a lot of this with children involved), they experienced one big emotional "ouch." Another person always seemed in bed with them, either Chad's or Marie's ex. As a result they never got their fresh start.

You may say that things like this shouldn't matter to strong people. If only human beings could be so strong. The problem is, they can't. It also buttresses God's argument against promiscuity, adultery and divorce.

Whenever men or women share intimacy with someone other than their lifetime spouse, the spectre of life-destroying insecurity is sown. Prudence would warn us to avoid this trap,

The New Start

and if not, keep it to an absolute minimum. But prudence doesn't always rule human behavior. The advice to courting couples is this: never, under any conditions, bring a former sexual partner into your relationship. Avoid all but the most necessary facts.

With each progressive relationship, whether it is the second boyfriend or the third husband, wouldn't it be wise to start from that moment on a new and clean beginning, to cut ties with the mistake-laden past and begin fresh, new and alive? If there was ever a perfect time for a new start, a new life, a white wedding, embarking on a new courting opportunity is it. Phil. 13:13, "Forgetting what is behind . . . " orders this and 2 Corinthians 5:17, ". . . the old is gone, the new has come!" declares it.

Woman, present yourself as a virgin with an unsoiled mind and spirit, no matter how life has treated you so far. Demonstrate to the world the redemptive power of Jesus Christ.

The male should present himself as a new man, a knight with new anointing and a new country. Together, make a pact for a fresh start where the past no longer exists and only the future counts. Heed Paul's words in Galatians 6:15, "What counts is the new creation."

What about the unavoidable, like when the ex-husband drops off the kids after his weekend of custody? The wise wife picks up them up instead. (This nuisance is well worth preserving the fresh start, isn't it?) What if the ex lives out of town, what then? The wise woman meets him at a pre-determined location.

What about phone calls? The responsible wife calls when the new spouse is absent, or handles the unavoidable call from another room with the door closed. She also allows for such necessary communication during specified hours, say eight to nine o'clock on Tuesdays or Thursdays. Whenever a spouse allows an ex-husband to intrude with at-will phone calls or visits, he remains a part of the new relationship.

What if your suitor asks you about your sexual past? Change subjects and explain why, while strongly suggesting he do the same. Enlighten him to the fresh start you are after. Or, just explain that it is a curse and move on.

You may say, isn't all this a bit unnecessary? The answer is, do you want a spotless, new relationship or do you want a contaminated one, however slight it may seem? Or, "My spouse can handle it." Perhaps he can, on the outside. Inside, he is being cheated out of an exclusive, whole and intact relationship. Instead of a new relationship, you risk giving him a split, fractured version that ruins quality. Don't sign him up for this and don't sign up for it yourself.

Perhaps it will help to look at it this way. Pretend that the topics, issues and possibilities for conversation comprise the longest smorgasbord of food you have ever seen. And it is a virgin smorgasbord, that is, you are the first one through the line. You see salads, vegetables, meat, fish, bread, deserts, all prepared in different ways. Would you want a plate of old garbage, rotting away, mixed in with that? The garbage is the past mistakes, past romances and sexual partners, now dead and stale. Perhaps it was once good food but now it needs to be removed and replaced.

Taking the example one step further, imagine the same food line after fifty people have passed through. The food is in disarray with messy spills and half empty containers. Can it be made virginous again? Of course! Clean it up, change the table cloth and put the leftover food in smaller containers. *Throw out the garbage.* Presto, a virgin smorgasbord! Now maintain the integrity of the virgin standard by tending to the dishes with care.

Look at it this way. It doesn't matter how many broken

The New Start

relationships you have had, how many mistakes you have made, how soiled your past is, or how old you are. More than anything, chastity, like holiness, is a state of mind, an alluring attitude, not a physical condition. With Christ, virginity can return overnight. If a carnal man can be born again, a woman can become a virgin again.

Endnotes

1. Prov. 6:26: "For the prostitute [sexual passion] reduces you to a loaf of bread . . ."
2. Hos. 4:11: "Harlotry, wine, and new wine take away the understanding." (NASV)

> *"Are you unmarried? Do not look for a [spouse]. But if you marry, you have not sinned; ... but those who marry will face many troubles in this life, and I want to spare you this."*
> —1 Corinthians 7:27-28.

15

Single Life

Imagine a situation where a woman has adapted successfully to a chaste, single life. That is, she is living out her covenant. She is in control of her flesh, and her urge to marry has been kept in proper perspective. Her single life is balanced with a couple close friends and several interesting companions. She has become culturally alive, learned the history of her region, has a volunteer schedule, has time for her remaining family, and exercises regularly. In addition, she has embraced a couple health fads and joined a local bicycle club. She uses her vacation time to travel. Saturday mornings are spent at garage sales, afternoons at a coffee house with a friend. Things like this surround her regular job, weekly church and Bible study, and she still has time left over. Money, as a single person, isn't a problem.

Single Life

Now imagine this woman trading in this life for a husband who, six months after the wedding, is revealed as a couch potato with a diminishing, and often crude, sex life. Along with this move, she has lost her ability to do things exactly as she wanted them, and it will not return. Her freedom is not just compromised, it is gone because freedom includes a peaceful state of mind. As for her former single life, she may as well have strapped a piano on her back and checked into a correctional facility for room and board. This is not as far-fetched as it sounds. Millions do it every year. Each of us knows someone who has done it. Sometimes, it is us.

How could anyone do such a thing? In a majority of cases it is for two reasons: loneliness and sex. The loneliness is caused by an immature, underdeveloped single life-style. The sex urge is caused by a passionate desire for something seemingly cosmic to spark up a dull, earthly existence.[1] Not realizing that sex, even with Mr. America, would one day lose its dream quality, the fool sells out her chance at an exciting single life for it.

God "gives" singleness as a gift. Don't turn in that gift on a husband until you've really thought it over. You will surrender a lot when you are married, or your marriage will be chaotic. Make sure you surrender to a worthy man. Whenever a woman contemplates marriage, she should compare a marriage to this person against the single life she has developed. In this way, a quality single life becomes a potent yardstick to measure what a man may offer her in marriage.[2]

Understand what you are giving up when you get married. Don't give up your right to make the final decision in your life to just anyone!

Failure to establish a mature single life has led to more careless character judgments, unfruitful relationships, and disastrous divorces than could be imagined. The aggrandizement of sex has claimed nearly as many. Any woman living an immature, stunted single life leaves out a valuable scale with which to weigh character as it must be weighed. She lacks the quality of life which allows her to say No! to draining life choices.[3] If her single life is asphyxiating, her mental state is too crippled to make a rational decision about marriage. She is too vulnerable to attacks of loneliness, or the allure of sex, or a persuasive personality. She is the one heading for disaster.

The earth is God's creation. This is America. The possibilities on this earth, in this country, in this age, are nearly *limitless*. Any woman over the age of consent who cannot develop a fruitful and fascinating single life in these circumstances is hardly marriage material herself.

Singles, begin today to cultivate a fascinating and mature single life. You need it for the clarity of mind necessary to say No! when your sifting turns up fool's gold. If you think that the idea of living is to get a husband as soon as you can because you are incomplete or odd without one, this kind of thinking is what keeps you from living now, away from what God has called you to be.

If you are single, you are not alone. Seventy million people in this country over the age of twenty-one are single! That is a "country" the size of New York, Michigan, Ohio, Pennsylvania, New Jersey, Massachusetts and Colorado combined! At the rate we are going, in fifty years there will be more single adults than married adults. Do you get the picture? You are not alone.

Just as God wants some to marry, he wants some to remain single. He wants them to live a life of abundance[4] as a powerful Christian testimony. If the world doesn't offer you a suitable spouse, it still offers a fascinating journey with unquenchable resources. I suggest that you, as a single woman, put your thoughts of marriage on the back burner and choose to enjoy the adventures of living as a child of God. Don't let opportunities for work, service or life pass you by because you are occupied with not being married.

The opportunities of single life are the most enriching discoveries a person can make.

Endnotes

1. Gal. 5:24: "Those who belong to Christ Jesus have crucified the sinful nature with its passions and desires." Tit. 3:3: "At one time we too were foolish . . . enslaved by all kinds of passions and pleasures."
2. Prov. 31:25: "She is clothed with strength and dignity; she can laugh at the days to come."
3. Js. 3:13 (reverse gender): "Who is wise and understanding among you? Let him show it by his good life . . ."
4. Jn. 10:10: "I have come that they may have life, and have it to the full."

> *"Wash and perfume yourself,
> and put on your best clothes."*
> —Ruth 3:3

16

In the Midst of Men

If you choose to pursue marriage, give God every chance to work with you. After all, the final decision is up to Him.

The smart cookie goes about cultivating an enriching single life, with the hobby of sifting men for someone capable of elevating it to an even higher level. All the candidates who are not capable are ruled out as husbands. If done correctly, her single life can not help but place her in the midst of several eligible men. This gives God every chance to work.

No greater example of placing one's self in the midst is that of Ruth and Naomi in the Book of Ruth. The Bible says that Boaz had seen Ruth, taken favorable note of her, but had done little about it. This is not unusual for men. Men can be so preoccupied with male "stuff" that they fail to recognize opportunity. In this case, Boaz was busy with his harvest. The women decided not to wait. Naomi went to work. She arranged to put Ruth at the feet of Boaz.

The Book of Ruth is not a story about two man-chasers. Quite the contrary. The wise woman quickly knows the difference between putting herself in the midst of men and chasing after them.

This raises the issue of "honorable pursuit." Honorable pursuit of the opposite sex is solely a matter of intent. Considering Ruth's bold example, a woman who sits on a bar stool next to a man in order to sift him for marital possibilities is more honorable in God's eyes than the wolf in sheep's clothing who sifts a church congregation for a vulnerable female whom he can adulterate. It is a matter of intent.

The wise man should place himself in enough social situations to allow a "midst" to exist. A wise woman seeks out these places and puts herself in them. However, she may become frustrated that men are not taking her bait. Perhaps God has placed a hedge of protection around her, keeping her from having a relationship, knowing that her spiritual condition is weak.[1] If God sees that your life is not yielded to Him, or hears you constantly recalling the past with bitterness, He could be waiting very patiently for you to change. If after an adequate (not agonizing) period of time has passed to rule out hedge protection, a Christian counselor specializing in this area should be hired to add another viewpoint. Many times he or she will be able to see obstructions or behavioral patterns which are foiling a woman's efforts.

Women should know that *good* men are not skirt-chasers, men whose midst is a twenty-four hour cafe. Good men are busy with other pursuits—performing well at work, studying spiritual matters, competing for an edge in the marketplace, tending to social obligations, exercising their maleness. Other "men things" like sports, hunting or fishing, the care of a house or automobile, sop up more brainwork. Good men are doing anything but "presenting themselves" around the clock.

How frustrating it must be for the woman who sees an opportunity, plans a brilliant strategy to put herself right on the X at the perfect time, only to see the man totally oblivious, walking away in a stupor, his mind on some distant river where the trout could be biting.

For many women, I would humbly suggest that the problem is not a lack of decent men, but an unwillingness to be realistic. Most women want happiness, but they look for excitement. They say they want a clean spirit but end up choosing flesh. They search for a man with an exciting job and exciting hobbies, even though they are not interested in becoming involved in either. They pass over stable men looking for a man who seems amusing and charming instead of someone who is caring, intelligent and solid. They want someone they can "click with" instantly, instead of realizing that durable relationships must be developed one day at a time. These women are more likely to wind up with an adventurer who wants sex and then will leave, rather than a loyal man who will take things slowly and remain devoted.

Women who complain that there are no good men out there should take a look at the ones they've passed up. That shy accountant with the thick glasses would unquestionably have made a better husband than the good-looking tennis pro, long on charm but short on character.

Spirituality must be first. It is the umbrella, and then there are things under that. If the umbrella isn't there, forget what the outer appearances of the guy might be. He might be a looker, a charmer, quite a talker, a doer, a go-getter—however, if the evidence of a strong walk with the Lord is not there, pass. There are good men, spiritual men; it is a matter of finding them.

No one said the game is easy, and getting started is sometimes the most difficult part. But for the Christian woman whose intent is honorable, honorable results can be expected.

Endnotes

1. Ac. 16:6-7: "Paul and his companions . . . having been kept by the Holy Spirit from preaching the word . . . they tried to enter Bithynia, but the Spirit of Jesus would not allow them to."

Appendix

Diary Helps

Many people resist keeping a journal because they think they aren't good enough writers, that someone will read their innermost thoughts or that they have more important things to do. Yet there are many powerful benefits, in addition to sifting male character. Among them are improved writing skills, healthy self-expression and stress reduction.

But more important to the courting woman, the journal/diary becomes a record of a man's oaths, a record of his compliance to those oaths, a record and description of confrontations to broken oaths, a record of his amends, a record of issues he avoids and a record of his solutions to his broken oaths. It is a record of the sifting process.

Often, a good diary reads like a straight line story which enables you to work out your sifting in an organized, step-by-step way. "Minutes" of conversations are all you need to keep track of the necessary information coming out of conversations.

Some people are inspired by an elegant bound notebook with fine paper, while others feel more comfortable letting the words flow onto loose-leaf sheets that can be clipped into a

Diary Helps

binder. Perhaps you prefer to record your thoughts on a computer. You can schedule twenty or thirty minutes with your journal at the same time each evening, or just pick up a pen when the mood strikes you.

Easy ways to start your entries:

1. Reread yesterday's entry as a springboard to today's entry.
2. Put yourself in the mood. Close your eyes, take a couple deep breaths. This focuses your thinking, clears a space in your mind and eases the transition from work day reality to contemplation. Ask yourself, "What am I feeling about this relationship at this moment?"
3. Jot down a few lines to summarize any progress on the relationship which happened today.
4. Perk your ears whenever you hear him begin a sentence beginning with "I" and record it, *He said* . . .
5. Prompt yourself with, "What will I get his word on tomorrow?"

To endure the assignment of recording your courtship:

1. Realize that diary-keeping is work. Emphasize the necessity of recording your courtship to the success of your life. Remind yourself of the value in finding the right spouse for you.
2. Remind yourself of the drama in recording history in the family tree.
3. Cue your purpose with questions like, "Why am I feeling so confused, angry, happy, encouraged, fearful? What's the most important thing that I need to clear up in this relationship?"

4. Constantly make and modify a master list of conversational topics from which to draw out his word. For a list, use any of the traits listed in Proverbs.
5. Freeze-frame oaths. Write a description of an oath that was truly revealing and memorable. Write it from his perspective, or start it with the words, *He said. . .* If it is something truly remarkable, make a note to bring it up again to make sure you and he have it in stone. You might cue it by saying, "Last week you said that. . . Did you really mean that?"
6. If you feel the need to confront something he has said but not done, write out how you will approach it and write in the expected outcome. The next entry, compare what you expected to what you got.
7. Create a list of topics for future conversations in red ink. This helps organize your conversations so that nothing of importance is left undiscussed.
8. Reread your journal constantly. This will help you spot areas left uncovered or up in the air.

Index

Abstinence 163
Adulterer 39
Angel's work 86, 88, 118, 165, 167
Angry Man 36, 38
Atonement 64
Avoiding issues 118, 121, 127
Bitterness,
　detecting personal 22
　remedy for 23
Boaz 178

Carnality,
　gauging in a man ... 160-62
Celibacy, romantic 25
Character,
　The Man of 34
　measure of 65
Clean heart 18
　recognizing 18
Cleaving 86, 160

Confrontation 137
　examples of 104, 109, 121, 134, 143, 147
　grading responses to 93
Conversations (courting)
　conducting your ... 99, 113
　examples 100
　one unbreakable rule .. 168
Courting 10, 158
Creeps, identifying the 36
Cruel Man, The 38

Dating, non-believers 160
Detachment 95
　late term 154
Detours (evading issues) 126
Diary Helps 182
Diary (journal) 57
　as an authority 58
　examples 58, 102, 112, 123, 124
　reasons for 58, 59, 69

185

Divorce ... 10, 11, 19, 23, 25, 32, 34, 39, 46, 89, 152, 158, 170, 176
Entry level,
   of relationships ... 138-141
Equation, character,
   of favorable men 41
Evasive tactics 122, 126

False repentance 93
Final analysis
   (of relationship) 151
Fool, the 36, 38
Formal confrontation
   (in relationships) . 146-150
Formal meetings 152
Foundations, five vital 75

Gathering vows (oaths) .. 117
Gentle confrontations 143
Good Man, the 35

Hostile reactions 127
Hot-tempered Man, the 38

Idyllic responses 130
Integrity, three lays of 68
Intellectualizing 131
Internship
   (in relationships) . 144-145

Killer one-liners 145

Lazy Man, the 38
Leverage,
   of single women 88-89
Lip service 93

Male character,
   foundations of 32
Male ego 44
   woman's effect on .. 46, 87
Man
   angry 38
   capable 36
   cruel 38
   good 35
   hot-tempered 38
   lazy 38
   naive 39
   of Character 34
   of Folly 40
   proud 39
   rebellious 37
   scoffer 36, 39
   slanderer 36, 39
   wicked 37
   wise 35
   womanizer 40
   worthless 39
Man's word 50, 53
   triggering a 53
McCartney, Bill 59
Measure of character, the . 67
Mossholder, Ray 163

Index

Naomi 178
Naive Man 37

Octopus effect 163, 164

Platitudes 132
Premarital sex,
    curse of 165
Promise Keepers 59
Protection, God's 22
Proud Man, the 36

Questions, effective yes
    and no 119

Rebellious Man, the 39
Recording oaths 57
Rules to Broken Oaths 95
Ruth 76, 79
    book of 179

Sacrifices, personal 21
Satan 79
Scriptural authority ... 19, 81, 84
Scriptural submission 19, 77
Scoffer, the 39
Secondary virginity
    (renewed chastity) 173
Self-defense 129
Self-disclosure 115

Sexual involvement 162, 164-165
Sexual Temptation,
    10 Ways to Handle 166
Sifting the male character 63
Single life 157, 174
Singleness (singlehood) 175, 175-177
Sins, personal 21
Slanderer, the 39
Spiritual rehabilitation 17
Spiritual surgery 24
Spiritual warfare 79

Toothless confrontations 140

Vague answers 127
Vignettes,
    Chad and Marie 169
    Jennifer and Carl 46
    Sandra 13, 51, 82, 97
Virginity 173
Vows, gathering 56

Wicked Man, the 37
Will of God, doing the 20
Wilson, P.B. 24
Wise Man, the 35
Womanizer, the 40
Worthless Man, the 39

Rob Ellis, M. Ed., is a writer and Christian counselor who resides in Grand Rapids, Michigan. *Sifting Men*, a book counseling Christian women on male character, is his fourth book. In addition to counseling and writing, Rob, a former professional baseball player, spends summers coaching for the Minnesota Twins.

To contact the author regarding Sifting Men Seminars, books and additional single life materials, call 800-642-0562.